A...**XIA BARRABLE** is an early years educator with a passion for tr... ating research into her practice, in the classroom and at hoi ... . Inspired by the ever-growing field of positive psychology, she ...listed the help of friend and neuroscientist Dr Jenny Barnett to w... e this book.

Hav... grown up in Greece and the UK, Alexia taught in prep sch... in London before returning to Greece to work in international... hools. She has lectured on the MA in Education for Duno... e University's Athens campus. Married to a fellow teacher, Alexi... ives in the mountains outside of Athens with her husband, their ... o sons and four dogs.

DR J... **NY BARNETT** is a neuroscientist interested in the application... of cognitive science to practical problems. Trained at Oxfo... Cambridge and Harvard Universities, Jenny is an honorary resea... ner at the University of Cambridge and has contributed to more... han fifty scientific papers investigating the causes of mental health ...nd illness.

GROWING UP HAPPY

Alexia Barrable and Dr Jenny Barnett

A HOW TO BOOK

ROBINSON

ROBINSON

First published in 2016 by Robinson

1 3 5 7 9 10 8 6 4 2

A CIP catalogue record for this book
is available from the British Library.

ISBN: 978-1-47213-679-4

Typeset in Avenir by Hewer Text UK Ltd, Edinburgh
Printed in Great Britain by Clays Ltd, St Ives plc

Papers used by Robinson are from well-managed forests and other responsible sources

MIX
Paper from
responsible sources
FSC® C104740

Robinson
An imprint of
Little, Brown Book Group
Carmelite House
50 Victoria Embankment

How To B ... rown Book
Group. We ... experience
of their su ... market and
its sug ... ks.co.uk

For the three men in my life: Duncan, Joe
and Oliver. You are my sunshine.
A.B.

For all the wonderful friends who not only do a great
job bringing up happy, creative, kind, thoughtful, joyful
children – but also let me borrow them from time to time.
J.B.

Acknowledgements

This book would not have been possible without the fabulous community of people who have helped along the way. They say it takes a village to raise a child, and the same seems to hold true about books too. So here is a big 'thank you' to our village.

Jenny and I have nothing but gratitude to all the people who embraced the idea from the beginning and helped us believe that it was possible. Friends, but also helpful critics all along the way, Marietta Papadatou-Pastou, Cordelia Madden, Phoebe Vayanou, Anna Touloumakos. The colleagues who have worked alongside me and taught me pretty much all I have learnt about teaching: Judi Korakaki, Tara Callow, Julie Chalikiopoulou and Sally-Ann Morris. All the mothers and fathers who have listened carefully, shared their experiences and given us advice, but also just been a source of inspiration all along the way. The Facebook group Foreign Mothers and Mothers-to-be in Athens, who were a constant source of advice and encouragement. My mum and dad, for a childhood full of wonder and happy memories. Swava Kowalik, who helped look after my two little ones in the final stages of the writing of this book. And of course the schools I have worked at, where children do grow up happy!

Finally my biggest thanks go to my family: my husband, Duncan, my rock and biggest cheerleader. My children, Joe and Oliver who have brought the most happiness into our lives, and who have patiently (and happily) endured me experimenting with all these happiness ideas on them!

Dr Jenny Barnett has been my best friend for the last twenty years and has enthusiastically taken up most of the crazy undertakings I have suggested. Our partnership in writing this book has only strengthened our friendship and we are already planning our next adventure together!

Alexia Barrable, October 2015

Contents

Foreword

By Alice Callahan, PhD, author of *The Science of Mom*

A week ago, my five-year-old daughter, Cee, and I headed together out for some afternoon exercise. She recently mastered riding a two-wheel bike, and she never turns down the chance to take it for a spin. I'm thrilled that I can run along with her and get some exercise and fresh air, too. We were just emerging from a busy holiday season of visiting with relatives and travelling, and she and I could both use some one-on-one time together. This was just what we needed, I thought.

Except that our hour out together was actually pretty miserable. Cee seemed to whine about everything: the bumpy street, the cold, my safety rules, that I was going too slow, and a few minutes later, that I was going too fast. I tried to stay cheerful, but I found that I couldn't turn her mood around. It was as if she was determined to be unhappy that afternoon.

That night, after tucking Cee and her little brother into bed, I started reading *Growing Up Happy*. On the first page, I read about Alexia Barrable and Jenny Barnett's inspiration for this book: that ultimately, what we parents all want most for our children is that they are happy.

Yes! Those words rang so true to me, especially after my experience with Cee that afternoon. What I wanted most for Cee was that she could live each day with a happy heart. On that bike ride, I hoped that she could enjoy the power of her legs rather than whine about feeling tired, see the beauty in the silvery grey of the afternoon rather than grumble about the cold, and feel gratitude for our companionship rather than grumpy about my rules.

As all parents know, our kids are never going to be happy all of the time, and making that our goal would only lead to frustration. We all have days when we feel like things just aren't going our way. That day, I let Cee have her grumpy afternoon, but once she was asleep, I was inspired to think about how we could cultivate more happiness in our family. *Growing Up Happy* came at just the right time for me.

What this book teaches us is that happiness doesn't just happen to us. It isn't something to sit around waiting for, like lucky fortune or good weather. It is something that we can create for ourselves and for our children. And even more importantly, we can teach them – mainly through our own example – how to create their *own* happiness, a skill set that will serve them throughout their lives.

xvi

At first glance, wishing our children to simply be happy might seem a bit shallow. It might conjure up mental pictures of a child getting every toy or treat that they request or having a life filled with fun experiences. Yet, we know from our own lives that having more things doesn't necessarily bring more happiness, and fun is just as much about our attitude as it is about a particular experience.

As we learn in *Growing Up Happy*, it turns out that the same things that make people happier also make them better citizens of the world, and that is far from a shallow wish for our children. Expressing gratitude, finding meaningful work, helping others, being mindful – these are all examples of practices that create happiness in an individual, but they also radiate out in ways that make the world around us better. Over time, they can become lifelong habits, *a way of being* that will help our children be resilient to hardship and disappointment and indeed live happy lives, even when they are no longer living under the same roof as us.

The authors of *Growing Up Happy* have done a tremendous service to parents and educators by sorting through the scientific research on happiness to identify evidence-based strategies for increasing it. Supported by science and tested in the classroom and home by one of the authors, this book is a treasure trove of ideas to try as you see what works best for the children in your life.

When caring for children, so much of our days are consumed in what can feel like mundane routines. There are constant cycles of diapering and dressing, cooking and cleaning up, playing and bathing, and waking up and winding down. How much can we infuse happiness into these routines?

This book has inspired me to start by focusing on a few small but significant moments in the day. I've set an intention to be sure that we start each day with a happy greeting, so that when my kids wake me in the morning (always too early!), I remember to pull them in for a hug and kiss and a few sweet words. Our whole family is enjoying a pause before we begin our evening meal to reflect on something we're feeling grateful for. And at the end of the day, as I tuck Cee into bed, I'm making it part of our routine to name our favourite part of the day, a way to recycle happiness and go to sleep thinking a happy thought.

There are many more ideas in *Growing Up Happy* that I'll be trying with my children. This book teaches us that small actions and little habits can go a long way towards making a happy day – and a happy childhood.

Introduction –

If You're Happy And You Know It . . .

'Happiness is the meaning and the purpose of life, the whole aim and end of human existence.'   *Aristotle*

'Happiness depends upon ourselves.'   *Aristotle*

How to Use this Book

This book is not a parenting manual. It will not tell you how to be a flawless parent, or how to raise perfect children, but it should give you some ideas on how to make the days you spend with your kids more enjoyable, meaningful and, ultimately, happier. It is an extended look into what makes children happy, and a journey exploring how what works in theory can best be applied in practice. It is also a record of how, over several years, I have worked to put happiness habits into action in my classroom and in my home. From this experience I can tell you one useful side-effect of using these techniques: the whole family benefits. Happiness is contagious!

The book was not written to be read from beginning to end in one single sitting. It is meant for busy parents of young kids who do not have the luxury of uninterrupted reading time. So, pick it up and put it down as you wish, open it on one chapter and skip another if you'd like: there is no correct way to read it and no particular order it should be read in. Dip in and out, try different things and see how these habits can work for you and your family.

Each chapter is broken up into sections. First we give a quick introduction to the happiness habit and take a look at the scientific research supporting the idea. Then there are two practical sections describing how I have put these habits into practice: in my professional life as a teacher, and then at home with my children. I've also included snippets from more experienced mothers than myself: often the most precious resource for practical solutions in my life are mothers who are ahead of me in the parenting game, who have been there and done it all before me! At the end of most chapters I have suggested some ways of using technology to get these happy habits into your life. If you are proud parents of slightly older kids you might find that this section can help get your children on board more easily.

The Idea

The idea for this book came to me before my first child. As the anticipation of looming motherhood engulfed me, thrilled me and scared me, often in equal measure, I wondered what I wanted for my future kids. What were my aspirations for them? As a seasoned education professional I had often heard parents speak about what they wanted for *their* children. It seemed to me that people often had strikingly diverse yet at the same time incredibly similar aspirations for their kids. When you truly boiled them down, when you got to their very essence, what people wanted for their kids could be summed up in one word: happiness. And so I too reached that conclusion, that the ultimate gift I wished upon my future children was the ability to be happy. Not simply to have fun, though that too can be a worthwhile goal, but to be happy in a deeper, meaningful, more fulfilled way.

At the same time the science of happiness and well-being, often called 'positive psychology', had really taken off. Led by Martin Seligman, there are now hundreds of scientists conducting research into the once-elusive field of happiness. They were, and are, learning many interesting things about happiness, some confirming what common sense or folk wisdom would already have you believe, but also with some rather surprising and counterintuitive conclusions too.

I have always been a believer of evidence-based practice, including in the field of education. At the time I was teaching full-time and felt there was a real opportunity to take some of that new research and apply it in my classroom, as well as draw from my ten-year experience of teaching young children. Later, once I became a full-time mum, I returned to the happiness literature and tried practising it at home with my kids, Joe my eldest and Oliver, who was born at the start of this project. My long-suffering husband, Duncan, was a good sport and joined in too!

To help make some sense of the ever-growing body of research, I enlisted the help of my friend Jenny, a psychologist and neuro-scientist who shares my passion for applying science to day-to-day life. Together we read and talked about countless pieces of research on well-being and happiness. Gradually we started collating a list of everyday practices that seemed to lead to enhanced well-being, a better mood, more enjoyable days and an overall more fulfilled life. The more we looked the more it became apparent that there was no big secret to happiness, except that it comes in many small ways, in distinct moments: an ice cream by the beach, the smell of freshly cut grass, a walk with the dogs, planning a surprise party. The happiest people seemed to be those who had worked out how to build up those small moments into an overarching theme in their life: into greater contentment, and a sense of purpose.

As we delved into the literature, we noticed that there were a few key habits that happy people tend to have. In a simplified way, we started thinking of happiness as a set of daily habits. We have tried to bring most of these things together in this book. However, the list is by no means exhaustive. The ten aspects of happiness that we discuss are merely suggestions that, adopted and used regularly, should boost your daily well-being.

Some of them will give you an instant mood boost (like Singing and Smiles), some can lead towards a life well lived (like Finding Meaning and Finding Flow). Some are small changes in your daily routine (like The Great Outdoors and Mindfulness) while others are a change of perspective (like Gratitude). At the heart of most of them are relationships and community: they will bring us closer together, as a family, and strengthen our social bonds. Finally, they are all supported by some amount of scientific evidence, which we have tried to lay out in a simple and easy to understand way.

Why Happiness?

I am often asked why I focus on children's happiness so much, rather than other life skills or academic success. There is a potential for misunderstanding here, so I always start by explaining what happiness means to me in simple terms. For me, and for the purposes of this book, happiness is both the joy of living (*joie de vivre*), which can be found in the little pleasures every day, but also and more importantly, the lasting sense of contentment that people have when they are leading a full life. Not full of material things, or hedonistic pursuits, but full of meaning, deep relationships and the pursuit of fulfilling activities. I believe that when this kind of happiness comes first, then other good things follow.

There is evidence for that too! Research suggests that happier pupils make better learners: they tend to be more motivated and stay focused for longer. There has been recent evidence to suggest that children as young as eighteen months learn better when laughter is involved. Happier pupils also tend to behave better in class, which can lead to a virtuous cycle of better learning for all.

Happy people are also kinder (and it seems that kinder people are happier too). They tend to have better health, live longer and have lasting relationships, which in turn makes them happier. And finally happy people tend to be more successful, because it seems that happiness inspires you to work hard now for a better future. So, although happiness is worth pursuing for its own sake, there are many additional benefits to being happy: all of them things that we parents wish for our kids!

An Overarching Theme

Humans are social animals. We have evolved to be part of a tribe, a village, and the fundamental human desire to belong is still strong. We seek to be part of groups, from smaller ones like couples and families, to larger ones, like churches, clubs and teams. It doesn't matter whether you are an introvert or extravert – social interaction, talking and being together make us happier.

Relationships with those around us are a major source of happiness (and occasional strife too, make no mistake!). As such, no book about well-being would be complete without acknowledging that. Yet, as you will see, there is no chapter dedicated specifically to socialising or building stronger connections to those around us. The reason is that strengthening relationships, within our families and beyond, is a theme that runs through every chapter of the book. Every happiness habit we discuss is in part about strengthening the connections between us, within our family and within our wider community. Activities like singing in a choir or volunteering will make us happy in part because through them we embed ourselves in the community, creating new networks and connections. When we create new family traditions, reminisce about shared experiences, or simply have regular meals or walks together, we are strengthening family bonds that promote long lasting well-being for every member of the family.

A Short but Important Note on Modelling

There have been numerous studies about how children learn from those around them, and one of the best ways is by copying what they see us adults do. This holds true in all walks of life, from eating behaviours, to kindness, from patience to dental hygiene. And here's something more: children don't just imitate the end result either, but they watch closely and tend to copy all of the actions that lead up to it. In fact, this characteristic of humans may well be one of the cornerstones of how culture gets transmitted. As a result, it is often useful to leave the explicit 'teaching' aside, and let our children do what they do best: absorb our habits of happiness by watching us practise them every day. If this leads to increased happiness and well-being for every single member of the family, that's definitely a win-win situation!

Disclaimer

This book draws upon the experience of over ten years of working with children, in various school settings. The situations written about in the book are a fictionalisation of real events, and the characters mentioned are composites of many of the pupils and teachers I have worked with over the years.

Smiles

'The shortest distance between two people is a smile.' *Anonymous*

 ## *The Idea*

We might not know *all* the good that a simple smile can do but we now know enough to say that smiling can actively boost our happiness. It's a two-way benefit: smiling improves our mood, but looking at smiling faces can also make us happier and more optimistic about the future. On top of that, smiling at others can make us seem more approachable and friendlier, giving us a social advantage too.

Common sense tells us that people who are happier smile more, but could it be that a smile is only the first part of a virtuous, happy cycle? Does a smile have to be genuine to benefit the mood of the giver or receiver? And how can we best nudge children towards simply smiling a little bit more?

The Research

Babies' smiles are one of the earliest rewards of parenting. In return, most babies see a higher proportion of smiling faces during their earliest months than they ever will again. What effect does this reciprocal smiling have, and when do babies start to understand what a smile means? Of course babies cannot tell us directly what they see or understand. But by studying what they choose to pay attention to, we have learnt a lot about how the developing brain and visual system lets babies learn about the significance of smiling faces.

At just a few days old, newborn babies prefer to look at faces than anything else, and by three months old, they can tell the difference between happy, surprised and angry faces. This is quite remarkable given how immature the visual system is at birth, and reflects just how important a cue faces are during development. By four months, babies prefer to look at happy faces than faces with other expressions. At around five months, they start to understand that two different people's happy faces are in some way similar, although they don't seem to learn about other categories of emotion for a couple more months, perhaps because they see more happy faces than any other kind. This categorisation is the beginning of the path to understanding that 'happy face' is a universal reaction to a particular kind of situation, teaching babies something about cause and effect in the world around them. By around one year, infants use other people's smiles and other facial expressions as 'social reference' cues, helping them interpret the emotional significance of events.

As language and other skills develop, smiles become just one of the child's tools to understand the world and express his or her own feelings. Young children quickly become adept at understanding and expressing feelings through words, tone of voice, body language and gestures. Yet facial expressions, particularly smiles, seem to retain a uniquely important role. We process them incredibly quickly: studies measuring the electrical activity of the brain show that it takes less than one-seventh of a second for the brain to respond to pictures of people smiling.

Facial expressions are also a key communication tool for our primate relatives, where the ability to express emotions vocally is limited. Primates 'smile' using a facial muscle structure that is almost identical to ours, producing a bare-toothed grin that is used to communicate and strengthen social bonds in just the same way as our smile.

So how does smiling more promote happiness? One way is that, when it comes to smiling, faking it really does make you feel better. In one classic psychology experiment, participants were asked to rate how funny different cartoons were while either holding a pencil between their front teeth – which forces a smile-like facial expression – or between their lips, which prevented them from smiling. As you'll have guessed, those with the pencil between their teeth found the cartoons funnier than those who were prevented from smiling. This is one example of a bigger truth: our psychological and cognitive experience of emotion is irrevocably mixed up with our physical, bodily experience.

Smiles are particularly important when dealing with kids because emotions are contagious. We often, unwittingly, mimic the facial expression and posture of someone we're talking to. People who get along well – such as partners in happy marriages – are more often seen to do this, while those who find social interactions more difficult, such as people with autism, do it less. In fact re-enacting the physical expression of someone else's emotion with our own body causes us to feel, psychologically, a little bit of their emotional state.

Recently it has been suggested that there may be specific neurons in the front part of our brain that are directly responsible for the effect that watching another person's action has on you. 'Mirror neurons' are nerve cells which fire both when you perform a specific action and when you see another person performing that action. Although discovered originally in primates, direct recordings from wires inserted into the brains of people who were having surgery for epilepsy suggest that they also exist in humans. Mirror neurons may be important in many aspects of our social development, including empathy and bonding: we know for example that we like people more if we imitate them. Mirror neurons may also be one of the means by which children can learn by watching others rather than through direct experience – something that could be helpful or unhelpful, depending on the model they are learning from!

Feeling an emotion yourself and recognising it in another person's expression are quite similar at the level of brain function. To demonstrate this, in one experiment participants underwent brain scanning while smelling a disgusting smell, and then again when watching a video of someone else expressing their disgust. The two experiences were found to activate much of the same neural circuitry. Other studies have shown that remembering an emotion activates much of the same system as experiencing it in the first place. This is probably why reliving emotional moments can be as intense as experiencing them for the first time (and why remembering happy times can be a considerable mood boost to kids and adults alike!).

Not all smiles denote happiness. Some people smile when they lie, when they flirt, are embarrassed or frightened. Paul Ekman, the psychologist who first documented how universal human facial expressions are, described seventeen additional types of smile. Faked smiles are relatively easy to detect, because they don't usually activate the cheek raiser muscle that creates crow's feet around the eyes. By looking at these muscles, experts can tell apart real 'Duchenne' smiles from fake ones. But even non-experts rate real smiles, and the people that give them, as more genuine, attractive and trustworthy.

So, smiling is definitely a good way to boost you and your kids' day. And if you really don't feel like smiling, it's probably worth faking it from time to time. It may well make you feel better, and at the worst you'll be helping children to become more skilful readers of their social world.

PRACTISING THE HAPPINESS HABIT

 At School

I'm a smiley person. Or maybe I should be a little more precise here: I never used to be a smiley person, but these last few years I have been consciously working at it and I am now a smile pro! Like anything else, smiling seems to be a habit, one which can have quite profound effects both on ourselves, and on how others perceive us. So it is not long before I decide to look into the 'where' and 'why' of my smiling habit and then try to see how I could encourage those around me to smile more too.

Taking a quick 'smile audit' I realise that I spend a lot of my time at school smiling. One of the reasons seems to be that I am responding to others' smiley faces with a smile of my own. The scientist in me is intrigued by the idea that looking at a smiley face might make us more likely to smile ourselves, so I decide to put it into practice: all I have to do is remember to smile more myself, then observe how my pupils respond. As I become aware of my own smiles, I notice that it's a rare occasion when someone does not return a smile. Wanting to make this habit stick, I try something sneaky: by linking it to another, more automatic activity I can multiply the frequency of my smiles, and consequently of those around me.

A smile trigger – the simple 'thank you'

Looking at my day I realise that the easiest action I can link my smile to is the humble 'thank you' I utter a hundred times each day. I notice that most of the time saying 'thank you' naturally comes with a smile anyway. All I have to do is use thank you as a trigger and make sure I always smile with it. Eye contact also helps, so I try to incorporate that into my routine. And I am right: it seems to me that smiling at people when saying 'thank you' triggers their own smiles too. Hardly surprising, but within a week it becomes ingrained. When I share this with the kids they are keen to try it too. In a matter of days I seem to be surrounded by smiles . . . and very polite children. We are on our way to the virtuous happiness cycle!

A joke a day

It is part of my class tradition to read a poem a day. It usually happens at the end of the day, or during lunchtime. What if, instead of poems, we read a joke? I think long and hard about it and for a special 'joke week' I introduce a joke a day in place of a poem a day. I take out one of the joke books from the library and simply take over the already established routine of the poem. I enjoy reading the jokes, as silly as they are, and the kids enjoy having an extra laugh.

I am a little sad, however. I do not want to lose my poetry moment: I am sure that the kids get a lot out of hearing a few verses every day. They understand some of the workings of language, see how rhyme and rhythm can be used, get familiar with scansion and this idiosyncratic way of expression called poetry. I do not want my pupils to miss out on all of these benefits.

Then Isobel gives me the answer. One day she brings into school Spike Milligan's *Silly Verse for Kids*. And just like that it seems we can combine both the benefits of poetry with the extra bonus of a laugh and smile. As we take in the absurd images that Spike Milligan presents to us, as we look at the silly illustrations, we laugh and laugh with our hearts and bellies. I am a happy teacher and the kids are elated too!

Practise smiles

Mary is a drama teacher and she has come to deliver a lesson to my class. She is tall and slender and dressed in arty, flowy clothes.

She looks like a serious artist, yet the minute she starts talking she is all silliness and the kids absolutely love her. I have asked to observe as she takes a drama class with my six year olds, and she has allowed me to, with one condition: I have to join in too! I don't have an actor's bone anywhere in my body, but I reluctantly agree – when else do I have the chance to watch a professional drama teacher deliver a lesson? If I am honest I am here to steal ideas, and Mary tells me she is happy to share them with me. With her fifteen years of experience I am certain she has many.

She sits down with the kids in a circle and the first thing they do is practise faces: a sad face, a happy face, a scared face and a surprised face. I notice that after each negative face Mary asks for a positive one. I join in, doing my best to smile and cry, to look surprised and angry. The next day I decide to bring the game into my class. But instead of general sad and happy faces, I want to see what happens when we are more specific: when I remind children of actual moments in their lives.

So we practise the 'Christmas morning face' and the 'Dad comes home after a trip away'. We get the 'you win a race at sports day' face and the 'puppy's first day home' face. We also get the 'your best friend doesn't want to play with you' face, but I try to keep a high ratio of happy to sad.

Soon enough the kids get into the swing of things and I ask them to leave me notes with ideas. I am so pleased to see 'tasting your own birthday cake' and 'bumping into your friends at the beach', as well as 'baking cookies with Grandma' and 'building a treehouse' as some of the suggestions that come my way. Linking these memories with expressions gives us all a happiness boost every day!

Smile buddies

With any habit that we try to learn, utilising our social group is a big help. I decide to take advantage of that and give each child a 'smile buddy' as another way to trigger these contagious smiles in class. At first I think I will ask the children to pair up with a smile buddy themselves, but then think better of it. I want to link together some children that do not normally get to interact all that much and so I decide to pick them myself. The idea is simple: every time you see your 'smile buddy' you try and give them a smile. You should aim to make the smile as genuine as possible: we practise some genuine smiles in the mirror, trying to get our eyes to smile as well as our mouths. (That exercise alone was quite mood-lifting!) If the other person forgets to smile back, you can give them a wink, as a reminder. If they still do not smile back, that is OK too; it is important to know that not everyone can be happy all the time. I stress to the kids that it is not a competition and it is not compulsory, it is just a game that we will play for the next few weeks.

Does it work? I think so – most children are very smiley anyway, and simply making eye contact or winking at each other increases the frequency of smiling within my class. Would I do it again? Actually, I am not sure that kids of this age need such an intervention – they seem to be social and smiley already and have increased their smiles by simply getting into the trigger word philosophy. Still, it is fun for a week or two and it brings some unlikely pairs closer together!

 At Home

Start your day with a smile

When my baby was about six months old he still spent the night in a cot attached to our spousal bed. Aside from the practical benefits of having him so close at night one of the reasons I loved having him there was the gummy smile I got every single morning.

There is something magical that happens in the life of a new parent around six weeks after the birth. Something that more than makes up for the sleepless nights and the copious nappies: the first smiles. Actually I don't remember his first smile, but I do remember the period in which he started smiling very distinctly. His smile made me smile. It still is one of the happiest memories of babyhood I keep close to my heart.

So I have tried to take this lesson from my baby: a day that starts with a smile is a happy one. I take his smile and raise him my own! I make a point to greet every member of the family with a smile first thing in the morning and, unsurprisingly, I get a smile back in return. I'm not sure if this increases my sons' well-being but I can feel my heart lift when we start our day like that.

Surrounded by smiles

Taking advantage of the research that suggests that even looking at smiley pictures can help us be more smiley and lift our moods, albeit fleetingly, I make a decision to add more portraits to our collection of pictures. It takes significant effort to find enough traditional smiley photos of the family as we so rarely get round to having prints made, but then I realise that some of our favourite family pictures are linked to this weird tradition that we have. We don't visit shopping malls often, but when we do go to one of the ones close to us we have set up a tradition that we take a photo in the photo booth that they have there. The pictures now span several years from when Duncan and I were a carefree couple, to the arrival of Joe and then Oliver, as well as some extra strips with much-loved family members and friends (we take our guests to the booth too). It is a wonderful collection and the pictures are all truly happiness-capturing. They are mostly of smiley faces, but also some silly faces too. I catch myself smiling at these pictures every time I see them, so I decide to put them somewhere prominent and share them with the kids often. On the fridge they go!

A ritual of happy thoughts

As I find myself more and more aware of when I smile (and when I don't) I realise that a lot of the time my smiles are not only connected to what is happening in the moment, but are also linked to happy memories. I take the thought a little further: there are things, actions and phrases that I associate with people I love: my dad's habit of drinking his coffee with a biscuit, my mum's way of washing her hands and splashing her face when it's hot, my grandmother's love for ice-cream cones and even Joe's loud 'click!' when I buckle his seatbelt. Thoughts of my loved ones pop into my head every time I do any of the above actions: have a coffee or an ice-cream cone, or buckle my own seatbelt, whether these people are there or not. The thought of them unfailingly puts a smile on my face. It is not difficult to share these thoughts with my kids, in the hope that they too associate an action with a loved one. It is easy and ends up being lots of fun. It is also a way for me to share with my kids family traditions and stories that would otherwise be lost for ever.

'This is the way Grandad used to drink his coffee' I say, dunking a biscuit into my drink and giving an exaggerated 'Mmmm'. Joe soon starts dipping his own rusk into his milk and saying

'Grandad!' It's like an inside joke, a family story and it always brings a smile to my face. Every time we have an ice-cream cone we share the same story of my grandmother, whom the kids will never meet, and her awe at the wonders of science that could produce such engineering feats as ice-cream cones. (My grandma really thought ice-cream cones were the pinnacle of food technology and commented on it every time she had one.) It is a great way to smile, share family stories and create our very own family traditions. I wonder what my kids will say about me one day!

 ## Tech it up

Smilefy your mobile phone: pick a picture of a loved one with a smile on their face and make it your screensaver on your mobile phone. Every time you look to see if there's a message, or even just look at the time, you should get a boost of happiness! On some phones you can go further and add pictures to your closest contacts – I have a lovely picture of my husband and youngest son set up so every time he calls they appear, all smiles.

Choose a joke app and put it on your mobile or tablet. You will get the joke of the day automatically to your device every morning and you can share a laugh with the whole family!

Gratitude

'Do not indulge in dreams of having what you have not,
but reckon up the chief of the blessings you do possess,
and then thankfully remember how you would crave
for them if they were not yours.' *Marcus Aurelius*

 ## The Idea

Which comes first, gratitude or happiness? Logically you might
think of gratitude as a by-product of being happy. After all, isn't it
easier to be grateful for what you have when you are happy?
This idea is ingrained in our culture; it is the basis of advertising
and consumerism: 'If only I had a new car I would be happy'. If we
could move to 'I am thankful for having a car' it would probably
have quite a knock-on effect on our buying habits – and our lives.
At the beginning of my journey in researching happiness, I quickly
became convinced that gratitude is one habit that can really
enhance my happiness. Of course, there is a difference between
realising, putting it into action, and making it into a habit! A few

months later, visiting an orphanage in Ethiopia, it became startlingly clear to me that, contrary to all of my expectations, the children seem very happy. One of the reasons I decided to write this book was the apparent difference in happiness between those kids, who lived in real poverty, and the children I knew back home, who lived in a very affluent environment. On reflection, it seemed to me that one of the main differences between those kids, and the kids I knew at home, was in gratitude.

I start by scrutinising my own behaviour. I started keeping a gratitude journal a few months before my visit to Ethiopia, in a bid to enjoy all the positives in my life, and to not take things for granted. I average about an entry a day, and I do find that I become better at it – the more I write and think about what I am grateful for, the more I start noticing things around me that I can be thankful for.

After my trip to Ethiopia, my gratitude entries multiply, to about three a day. Not only that, but their very nature changes. I start recording things like: 'I am grateful for the roof over my head' or 'I am grateful for the food on my table', whereas before, these things would never have crossed my mind – I was taking them for granted. Did I feel happier in those months too? I definitely think so – I think I appreciated the immense wealth I had a lot more and became more aware of just how lucky I was.

As a trip to a developing country is not feasible for everyone, I start thinking about how gratitude can be encouraged in all of our daily lives. How can we bring it into our own everyday habits and how can we get our children into the habit of being thankful? How much gratitude is needed and what is the best way to practise it?

The Research

People who express more gratitude tend to report being happier, more hopeful and more energetic, and less depressed, lonely and anxious. In other words, gratitude seems to be associated with emotional resilience. It has also been shown to go along with behaviours and attitudes that we might want to cultivate in children, such as being less materialistic, and more helpful, empathic and forgiving.

Showing that we are grateful seems to make us happy. In one survey, more than 90 per cent of adults and teenagers said that expressing gratitude made them extremely or somewhat happy. While this is great news, it is nonetheless difficult to be sure whether gratitude causes happiness or the other way round. It is also possible that a third factor causes both gratitude and happiness (or all of these things may be true!).

One useful way to tease apart these options is to look at what happens when people are randomly assigned to either increase their expressions of gratitude, or take part in some other activity. Gratitude interventions are quite commonly used by clinical psychologists when they are working with people experiencing a wide range of emotional problems, depression and anxiety disorders. As a result, there have now been many rigorous scientific studies which directly compare the effects on happiness of gratitude-based activities and other therapeutic techniques. The most common techniques used to increase gratitude are regularly writing a list or keeping a diary of things to be grateful for, most often listing three things every night before bed. This has been shown in several studies to be an effective way of improving positive emotions and decreasing negative ones. Importantly, people who are randomly assigned to the gratitude intervention tend to find it enjoyable and helpful – which is crucial if this is to become embedded as a happiness habit.

So research backs up the idea that actively practising gratitude increases your happiness, at least in the short term. There are several simple mechanisms by which this may happen: dwelling on positive things might increase feelings of happiness, spending more time thinking pleasant thoughts might leave less room for negative ones, and reflecting on ways in which you are lucky probably reduces the tendency to compare yourself negatively with other people.

Gratitude is also an important part of forming and strengthening relationships, which is a running theme throughout this book. The tendency to express gratitude in a relationship is correlated with the things that we value most in relationships, including the willingness to forgive, to find ways to resolve disagreements and to help one another.

The majority of these studies have been carried out in adults. Yet it is reasonable to think that children would see the same benefits from practising gratitude, and this is supported by the small number of studies where gratitude interventions have been adapted for use in schools with children and teenagers. In one study, classes of teenagers were assigned to either making a gratitude list, a list of daily hassles or no list each day for two weeks. Those in the gratitude classes reported finding school more satisfying and enjoyable at the end of the period, and that they learnt more than those in the other two groups. Compared with the daily hassle group they also reported increased well-being, and these differences were still visible when the classes were followed up three weeks later.

In another study, young people were assigned to either write about daily events or to take part in a 'gratitude visit', a face-to-face meeting where they expressed gratitude to someone who had had a positive effect on their life. Interestingly, those who benefited most from the gratitude visit were the young people who had reported being the least happy at the start of the study. While more research needs to be done in children, it certainly seems that practising gratitude can produce a meaningful increase in young people's happiness, and that those with the biggest need may be the most likely to benefit.

PRACTISING THE HAPPINESS HABIT

 ## *At School*

The great thing about gratitude is that it is one of the easiest habits to practise. Inspired by the above research, I decide to keep a gratitude journal with my class. At the end of each day we make a little time to jot down in our writing book three things that we are grateful for that day. It seems simple, not too time-consuming, and links in with some of our literacy targets. A win all round.

What is gratitude?

And yet, when I introduce the idea to a class of seven year olds, I am met with complete silence. I realise that part of the problem is semantics – the children simply don't seem to understand the word 'gratitude', or perhaps have little grasp of the concept.

'We will be thinking about all the things we are thankful for,' I rephrase.

Again I am met with blank stares. I give them a few examples, yet still the look of recognition I expect does not come. It becomes painfully obvious that most of the children I have in front of me are simply not familiar with the concept of gratitude. And so we all embark on a journey that is to be a little longer than I had initially anticipated.

I go home that night quite disheartened. I have to find a way to not only *practise* gratitude with these kids, but to *teach* them how to be grateful and what to be grateful for. Any educator (and parent) would probably agree that one of the easiest and most effective ways to teach children a concept is through modelling it. Modelling is when someone's behaviour changes as a result of observing the actions of another. I decide that for the next week I will model gratitude repetitively. Even if nothing else comes out of the exercise, the evidence suggests I will end up happier . . . It is worth a go!

The gratitude tree

The first thing to do is to work out how to record gratitude. After much thought I decide that I want something visual and something that the children are familiar with. In my class I have been growing an 'I Can Tree'. Well, from Monday morning, my 'I Can Tree' will start growing gratitude leaves. I choose the tree, because the children are already in the habit of making leaves, writing down what skills they have mastered each week, and putting them up on the tree, so I hope that they will be just as keen to add 'gratitude leaves' to it. I also think that having a visible symbol of our growing gratitude will be beneficial, plus the children can go back to it and read each other's entries – and mine, of course.

The first step to being thankful is recognising that what you have is a gift

The above becomes my motto, while I try to model gratitude for the kids.

On Monday morning, I start, very visibly, to write and display the things that I am grateful for. 'I am thankful for all the smiley faces in the room today' reads my very first leaf. Then the next one: 'I am thankful for the yummy chocolates that Molly gave out' (I want to draw attention to the small things that we can be thankful for and that we often take for granted). Slowly, some of the children start chipping in. 'I am thankful that it is my birthday today' and 'I am thankful for my presents' start appearing. 'I am thankful for my iPad' also appears on the tree. Very early on I make a pact with myself not to give any negative feedback regarding the gratitude statements the children decide to put up. It is important that they can share all of their feelings of gratitude, whether they are towards a person, an object or a situation.

At the end of the week we have quite a few leaves up. I make sure that we read them often and we celebrate each one for its own merit. I keep on modelling the habit of gratitude, by regularly making my own leaves and placing them up. If nothing else, it is certainly making me notice the good things in my life!

About three weeks in, something wonderful happens. I start noticing that the children are not only putting more leaves up, but they are putting up a lot more statements of gratitude about each other and about me. ('I am thankful for having you as a teacher' comes up, although it is followed by 'because you are the second best teacher in the school!') Our tree is filling up. It is looking lush! And, as we are actively looking for things to be grateful for, it is becoming very clear that we *do* have a lot of things to be grateful for.

After the Christmas break, and as the new year starts, we decide to put up one statement each, about something from the past year that we are grateful for. Most children find that easy, but I notice Felix, whose parents split up in the last year, is finding it hard. I go up to him and ask him about it.

'How is it going? Have you found something positive about last year?' I start.

He shakes his head and I can tell he is upset.

'It wasn't a great year for you, was it?' I feel I need to acknowledge this. The gratitude exercise is certainly not about denying our hardships, or even about finding silver linings in everything, but more about looking for the positives in our lives.

'It was a pretty rough year,' he smiles.

'Is there anything that we can be thankful for?' I gently prompt.

He takes a while to think of something. I leave him and walk around, reading everyone else's leaves in the process. Soon Felix comes up to me, a leaf in his hand. He smiles at me and shows me his leaf: 'I am thankful that last year is over!' He looks up at me. I take the pen and add: 'A brand new year is about to start!'

 ## At Home

Being thankful for our meals

I was not brought up in a religious home, so we never said grace at the table, but the more I read about gratitude, the more convinced I become that making a statement of thankfulness at each mealtime is an easy, poignant way to add gratitude into our busy schedule.

In my meditation practice (of which more later), I have used a gratitude exercise that makes me feel connected and at ease with the world. I decide to bring this sort of gratitude to our family breakfast table.

Breakfast for us tends to be the one meal that we try to have as a family. As my husband often works late, and my sons have a much earlier bedtime than we do, lunch and dinner tend to be fragmented during the week. But breakfast is something that we set aside to do as a family.

We try and make gratitude pervade each part of the breakfast process, a different one each day. On Monday, as I put the bread in the toaster we talk about how it is made of wheat and just how many people – the farmers, the factory workers, the lorry drivers, the supermarket stackers, the cashiers – have worked so that we can enjoy this loaf of bread at home.

On Wednesday we thank the cows for giving us the milk we drink, and on Thursday the chickens for laying the eggs we have. Some days we thank the bees that make the honey that we so enjoy! This is not time for feeling guilty about ethical farming practices (although I will, at some point, also discuss these with the kids) but it is a time to simply feel, and express, gratitude.

My eldest son absolutely loves this practice. I try not to overload our breakfast, but every day we think of something else to give thanks for. It makes me a lot more mindful of what we consume and it certainly starts our day with a very positive vibe!

Tidy-up gratitude

While searching for ways to add being grateful to our daily routine, I realise just how much of my day with small children involves tidying up and putting things away. We regularly sing while doing it, but oftentimes children find tidying boring. I decide that this is an ideal time to chat about just how grateful we should be for all the things that we have. I start it while we are putting the washing away. With each item of clothing I try and remind my sons (and myself) of where it has come from, and we give gratitude. It helps that 90 per cent of the boys' clothes have come from generous donations of friends whose kids have grown out of their clothes, and so we bring to mind each and every one who has given us these clothes.

'This T-shirt used to be Billy's,' I share with Joe. 'Thank you, Billy, for giving us this super T-shirt!'

We continue like that and they love finding out about each item. 'These shorts were a gift from Grandma,' and 'This T-shirt your uncle brought from South Africa. Thank you Grandma, thank you Uncle.' As we fold away the clothes he picks up a shirt and gives it to me. It is one of the shirts that no longer fit him and has been handed down to his little brother. I make sure I say a big 'thank you' to Joe for generously giving his brother some of his old clothes. He is beaming!

The routine soon rubs off on our general tidying up. Although we do not do it for every single item, quite often I remind him just how lucky we are to have all these toys in our home. And we truly are – I cannot easily forget some of the children we met in Ethiopia, whose only toys were the plastic tops of formula tins. In many ways perspective gives gratitude.

Our gratitude Christmas tree

I am very keen to somehow transfer the success of the gratitude tree from my classroom to my home, but I am hesitant. For one, I have no display board. On top of that, I don't want to have more clutter in my house or make more work for myself: as a mum of two young boys I am busy enough as is. But as Christmas approaches I see an opportunity! On top of our normal Christmas decorations, this year we will be hanging some gratitude ornaments on our tree. I buy some silver and gold card and cut it out into circles. With a non-erasable marker pen (which I guard with my life in case my toddler finds and uses it to decorate my walls and soft furnishings) we sit down each night before bedtime story and add a couple more things to our tree. It seems to become easier with every night we practise, and after a few days my eldest starts offering gratitude at other times of day, in order to remind me to put them up that night. After a particularly fun playdate, he reminds me that we have to write how thankful we are for having friends over. I wholeheartedly agree with him! Soon our tree is full of gratitude and, at this special time of year, we are ever so thankful to be so wealthy in friends, family, experiences and fun!

 ## Tech it up

There are some superb gratitude apps available, helping you keep a journal on your phone or tablet, as well as adding notes and photos to it. I kept an electronic gratitude journal for a year and loved looking back over it at the end.

Singing

'He who sings scares away his
woes.' *Miguel de Cervantes Saavedra*

 ## *The Idea*

Singing is present in all human cultures, and indeed in many
animal species, including birds, whales and gibbons. In
humans, singing is one of the activities – like laughter, crying
and speech – understood as ancient and universal. In most
cultures it is linked with rites of passage: marriages and
funerals, births and deaths.

Maternal singing is also a universal characteristic of humans, and
studies suggest that even very young infants respond more
strongly to a mother's song than to her speech. So it seems we
like being sung to, right from early infancy.

Does singing really make us happier, or is it just that the happier we are, the more likely we are to sing? And how can it best be added to our busy daily routine?

The Research

Does singing cause happiness? Studies in many different countries have found that people who sing in choirs report that it helps their mental and physical health and quality of life. Of course, there may be lots of other people who don't find that to be the case – and if they join a choir, they probably don't stay long!

Singing in a choir is a social activity, so it may help well-being by increasing a sense of community engagement, especially in people at risk of social isolation. In elderly people, for example, singing seems to not only improve self-reported well-being, but also to improve health more broadly. For example, it has been reported that older people who sing make fewer visits to the doctor, use less medication and experience fewer falls.

Singing is one of a range of creative after-school activities that parents often want, or feel obliged, to involve their children in. Is it worth it? On the one hand, there is evidence from large-scale studies that participating in such activities has a positive effect on young people's social and educational attainment. On the other hand, there are several reasons to view such studies with some caution.

First, just like with the adult choir-goers, it's likely that only those children who enjoy an activity will stick with it, while other children might not find that particular activity beneficial. Second, children who are encouraged to go to after-school clubs probably have other advantages – such as parents who have the time and interest to enrol them in these activities. As such it is hard to know whether the children are benefiting directly from the creative activity itself, or from these other factors.

Despite these caveats, it is consistently reported that taking part in singing and other creative activities increases confidence and self-esteem not only in socially advantaged but also in disadvantaged young people, suggesting that it is likely to have some true positive effect.

There are also potential physical benefits to singing. In adults with respiratory illnesses, singing helps improve breathing, which in turn improves quality of life. Singing is used as a therapeutic technique to help people suffering from a range of conditions which can affect communication or emotions, including Parkinson's disease and dementias, and has been shown to help people who have been paralysed to improve their breathing, voice control and speech.

Another physical effect of singing is that it releases endorphins, natural chemicals which reduce pain and can increase feelings of well-being. In one study, researchers studied how people's

39

pain thresholds were changed by taking part in different musical activities. They found that people could tolerate more pain, and reported being in a better mood, immediately after actively performing (through singing, dancing or drumming) than after taking part in low energy musical activities or just listening to music. Endorphins are not the only chemicals released by singing. Other researchers have reported that singing increases levels of oxytocin, a hormone involved in social bonding, and decreases cortisol, which is involved in regulating stress.

So taken together the evidence suggests that the choir singers may well be right that singing is making them happier, and possibly healthier too.

PRACTISING THE HAPPINESS HABIT

 At School

During my first year of teaching, in the middle of a Shrove Tuesday assembly, singing along to 'Toss the Pancake' (complete with actions), it hit me. Right there, in the full hall amongst two hundred kids, I realised in a somewhat transcendental moment, that I was so extremely happy to be a teacher, and spend my mornings singing at the top of my lungs, surrounded by happy children, and get paid for the privilege.

In my first class we sang regularly and even had a 'pick the tune' time at the end of each day, when a child, as a treat or a reward, was allowed to choose the song we would sing the next day. We would practise it right there and then, and in the process end our day on a high!

Later, when I moved to a bigger school, with a dedicated music department and separate music lessons, I lost the pleasure of singing in my classroom. Although recently, I sought it out again with my class in the build-up to Christmas.

A happy singalong

It begins when one of the girls in my class, inspired by her lunchtime choir practice, starts singing during an art lesson. Now, my normal response would be to ask her to stop, or possibly tap her gently on the shoulder. But this time, much to the surprise of the rest of my class, I join in. Encouraged by my unusual behaviour, more and more children join us, until the whole class is rocking to 'Deck the Halls'.

In reality this is just a one-off and events like this do not happen often. The thing is, schools are very busy places and time is at a premium. Not only that, but in the primary classroom there are often several activities going on at once: one group might have started an art activity, while another are finishing their writing and a third group are doing some group reading. Breaking into song, as nice as it would be, is generally not acceptable as it can disturb others.

However, there are some dead times in the day when singing can be used, not only to improve the general mood, but also with a purpose and to the advantage of the teacher.

Transition singing

Transition singing is something I use a lot in my class. A few verses of 'Are you listening to me?' (sung to the tune of 'Happy Birthday') can be used to help get the children's attention while they are absorbed in a task. Then, when their attention is all mine, I can redirect it to the next task on our schedule.

The advantages of singing instead of shouting or clapping to get the attention of more than twenty children in the tumult of a classroom are obvious, especially if you teach the children to respond with 'We are listening to you' sung to the same tune. Who doesn't want to put their pencil down and break into song? By joining in, the kids are much more likely to pause briefly in whatever it is they are doing and it gives us all a feel-good boost.

Once they have responded and I know that they are listening I can then speak to them in a lower tone and calmly, instead of shouting to be heard over the naturally noisy environment that the primary classroom should be.

I wonder if I can use transition singing in other ways too. One of the ways is to assign a tune to each transition activity. For example in one of my classes we had the 'line-up song' and the 'carpet song'. When I start singing one of the pre-assigned tunes the children follow by joining in, while at the same time walking to the line or to the carpet. Surprisingly, I find this technique results in fewer squabbles in the line and seems a more fun and quiet way to line up than my previous method, a countdown, most often rushed, which seemed to stress everyone out. Success!

Seeing as most of the kids find singing pleasurable and most kids love joining in a good singalong, as a canny teacher I decide to pair it together with another, not-so-pleasant activity, like tidying up. In one class I used to teach I found that tidying up was a particularly difficult activity. Children found the transition from playing to tidying up hard (do you blame them?) and I found that I had to go round and remind them that playing time was over for several minutes, and that tidying up was everyone's responsibility. A more experienced teacher saved me and in the process added one more song to my repertoire by suggesting that I prompted the children with the 'tidy up' song.

The simple song of 'If you're happy and you know it' slightly altered, so that in the third stanza you sing 'If you're happy and you know it . . . tidy up' fixed my problem and added a fun way to tidy up, while sharing a singalong with my class. The children tended to respond a lot better to this transition and enjoyed singing while they tidied up. This is definitely one that can also be used at home.

Pick the tune

I find that a lot of children enjoy being in control of the songs we all sing. When I ask the class which song we should sing, I soon realise that children place great significance on being the one to choose the tune! So I make up a new rule: each Friday towards the end of the day, one of the children in my class has the honour of picking two tunes. It is a great reward or a treat, so I make a point of choosing someone who has sung beautifully or with increased gusto during the week, or maybe a child who has been increasingly willing to tidy up during our 'tidy up song' or to sing and line up during one of our transition songs. That child gets to pick both tunes that we will then sing throughout the coming week. The songs go on my whiteboard and we practise singing them, with children moving from the carpet to the line, to their desk to their carpet, as I lead and they follow. The children enjoy this a lot, finding it extremely funny at times. It ends our weeks on a high.

As singing becomes a real treat for everyone and an integral part of our routine I come to notice a great thing about it: children are not too bothered about whether you can carry a tune or not. In fact, now that I think about it, it might even be the best thing about singing with children. I have never enjoyed singing as much as when I am surrounded by seven year olds and can sing with true abandon!

 ## At Home

I have never been a big singer, partly because my voice leaves a lot to be desired and partly because I grew up in a household and with a family who hardly sang. However, due to my job, I have a wealth of nursery rhymes stored up and waiting for the arrival of my own children.

A song for every occasion

So when that time comes and my kids are young, I am pleasantly surprised to find just how easily I can incorporate singing into my days with them. It is certainly a lot easier than trying to find time during a busy school day. We can sing in the morning over breakfast, during nappy changes, there is definitely singing in the bath and, much to my husband's dismay, the car is also a prime singing spot.

I find that singing becomes a lot more than just a fun activity: it is a lullaby, a 'feel-better' cue after a grazed knee, a way to help my sons learn to wait and a distinct code of communication between me and my boys. For example, my eldest quite quickly learns that when I start singing

'One, two, three, four, five,
Once I caught a fish alive'

it means he has to wait for something. Once he is old enough to join in he does, making the wait pass more quickly.

We have a bath song and a nappy changing song, and there is a lullaby that only Mum sings. By building up these routines around singing not only are we increasing our happiness, but I am helping teach my children how to deal with transitions better.

Transitions can be a difficult time at home as well as in the classroom, especially for toddlers. Anyone who has tried to get their three year old to put the Lego away and start the bedtime routine knows that full well. By adding singing to our transitions we lighten the mood and make it a little more enjoyable. Activities such as getting dressed, tidying up or driving have their own song associated with them. It can be a special 'tidy up' song, as above, or the children can pick their very own tune each week or month. I have found that if we stick to one tune per task, both the boys quickly learn what each song means.

Dressing time

Getting children dressed in the morning can be quite a stressful activity (for the parent, at least), especially when we are running late, so I decide that, on the mornings when we have adequate amounts of time, some singing might elevate our mood. The added bonus is that it helps my sons learn the names of the clothes as we put them on. (I often need to repeat verses several times while putting each garment on.) To the tune of 'The farmer's in his den' we sing a line for each item of clothing worn:

> 'I'm putting on my shirt,
> I'm putting on my shirt,
> Ee-i, ee-i,
> I'm putting on my shirt.
>
> I'm putting trousers on,
> I'm putting trousers on,
> Ee-i, ee-i,
> I'm putting trousers on.'

And so on until we are all dressed and ready to go! I am surprised (and secretly delighted) when I catch my son humming the song while I get his brother dressed.

Car journeys

Singing in the car can definitely be a good way to pass the time, as well as feel better. For those of us who are not experts in nursery rhymes, a CD with the most basic ones can lead the way. And when you get too tired of singing you can simply listen, while your little ones continue singing their hearts out.

Singing does not come naturally to everyone. I know that some people feel self-conscious when singing and others simply don't find it fun. My husband is one of those people and, despite my encouragement to sing with our boys he never feels comfortable doing so. Scheduling in a sing-and-dance-along to our week, usually on a Wednesday afternoon after school, gives us all a regular boost. We find a pop song we all like (the current favourite seems to be Pharrell's 'Happy') and let it play on repeat, while we all join in, some with singing and others with (silly) dancing. The goofier, the better! This should work with older children too, and the added movement should lift everyone's mood!

 Tech it up

My friend Gina, mum of two, tells me that an evening of karaoke can be a sure-fire way of getting some laughs, bonding and enjoying the benefits of singing. You don't need a real karaoke machine – a tablet or a computer with access to the internet will give you plenty of songs with lyrics to choose from. Just make sure the neighbours have been warned and don't expect your teenagers to be as forgiving with your vocal talents as your toddlers were . . .

Finding Meaning

'For it is in giving that we receive.' *Saint Francis of Assisi*

'If you knew what I know about the power of giving, you would not let a single meal pass without sharing it in some way.' *Buddha*

 The Idea

The true nature of happiness is often discussed but rarely agreed upon. It is elusive and multi-faceted. It is not simply about having fun, not just about enjoying ourselves. Adult humans look for and find meaning in their lives, and children, it seems, are no different.

In many developing countries children have no choice but to work for, or otherwise serve, the families and communities they live in. Serving others is something that is thought to increase our happiness at a deep level yet, in an effort to let our children enjoy their childhoods, we can sometimes risk depriving them of this opportunity to find a deeper sense of meaning in everyday life. There can be a real satisfaction in knowing that your actions are in some way making a difference in someone else's life – that you are an integral part of something bigger than yourself.

But here lies a challenge: how do we add meaning and purpose to our children's lives without overburdening them with responsibility? Are there simple ways we can incorporate meaningful activities into our and our children's days?

The Research

Most people would agree that today's children have fewer responsibilities than their grandparents did, and that the extent to which children are asked to undertake responsibilities such as doing chores and providing services varies hugely between cultures. A recent analysis of advice articles published in *Parents*, a popular American magazine, illustrates this nicely. In the 1930s to 1950s, articles discussed children being responsible for chores like preparing the family's meals, doing the household accounts, looking after sick relatives and mending furniture. In one letter from the 1930s a mother describes how she taught her four-year-old to lay kindling and light the fire so that the mother could get on with the cooking! But more recent articles were much more concerned with children's schoolwork, urging parents to give children relatively minor tasks such as feeding pets or laying the table, and often discussing how best to motivate and reward them for doing so. Based on these articles, American children today bear less family and societal responsibility than any children have ever done.

When you do someone a favour, it costs you time and effort that you could have put to doing something for yourself. So doing something that is selflessly helpful ('altruistic') is at a first glance something which makes no evolutionary sense. But you might point out that there are actually lots of selfish reasons for altruistic behaviour: it makes you look good in someone else's eyes, it makes you feel good about yourself and the person you helped will owe you a favour. The selfish gene argument says that, if the person that you are helping is someone you are related to, then helping them is also helping to pass on the genes you have in common.

These all seem like good reasons to be helpful – but how exactly can being helpful increase happiness? One way is that helping others activates the same brain circuits that are activated when we receive a reward or experience pleasure. To put it simply, doing something good for someone else feels a lot like having something good happen to us.

Children are inclined to be helpful from an early age, even if they do not receive rewards for this. Experiments have shown that toddlers will spontaneously help strangers by doing things like

53

picking up and returning a dropped book, even if they have to give up some fun activity to do so. In fact very young children spontaneously do things like sharing, comforting and helping people achieve their goals. Even before they are physically able to help, babies as young as six months can tell the difference between objects that are 'helping' versus 'hindering' others. And toddlers are also surprisingly generous, with studies reporting that before the age of two, children show greater happiness when they give than receive treats.

In most families, older siblings will help care for their younger brothers and sisters and, as long as it isn't too tiring or time-consuming, this benefits both kids. Older children who provide some care giving and teaching for their younger siblings tend to score better on reading and language tests, and both older and younger siblings seem to learn useful lessons about how to balance their own needs and feelings with those of others.

As children get older, the nature of their opportunities to care, be responsible and generous changes. Opportunities to be generous shift from sharing toys and treats to giving spare time and money for good. Most adults say they experience pleasure from activities like volunteering, doing random acts of kindness or spending money on others. It turns out we get much more pleasure from these acts if there is a social element in them. For example, giving money to a good cause feels best when it involves a social inter-action with someone directly connected to the cause. So the best way to encourage helpful behaviour in children may be to make it socially rewarding and to maximise the opportunity for interaction between the helper and the recipient of the help – be that another child, a family member or a teacher.

PRACTISING THE HAPPINESS HABIT

 At School

Zoe is walking down the corridor full of purpose. She is holding a bunch of papers tightly to her chest. Zoe is what many teachers would privately characterise as 'difficult'. She has a troubled background and chaotic family life and, at the age of eight, is often involved in fights in and out of school.

Yet, give her a job and she jumps at the opportunity to be helpful. She is, in fact, one of my most-used helpers. It starts with me sending her on errands simply to give her (and me) a break from the classroom, a chance to have a breath and an opportunity to calm any tensions. What I find, though, is that Zoe's mood instantly improves, after being helpful like that. She returns to class having a completely different approach to things and is even able to work cooperatively with others, something she usually finds challenging, to say the least. There is a deeper satisfaction she gains from being part of the community like that – it adds value to the picture she has of herself and she takes pride in her actions in relation to serving her classmates. I vow to build in some routines to add this kind of meaning to all of my pupils!

Monitors

Primary school teachers have known for years that most children respond very well to being given jobs. In my class I have several chores that are shared amongst the children in the class. I, like many other teachers, have a monitor chart pinned to our board and children's names rotate on a weekly basis. Jobs include taking the register to the secretary, helping people line up, making sure chairs are properly tucked in so as no one trips and an eco-monitor, in charge of the recycling.

The benefits are many: being a monitor gives children a boost in their self-esteem, makes them feel more connected to the whole and keeps them out of trouble. Children, when given responsibility for something and when they feel that they are trusted to do something well, rarely let me or the group down. Even children like Zoe, who often mess around, or inadvertently get 'lost' when walking around school, seem to find such chores meaningful and fulfilling.

I need to take this a step further. If finding meaning is about looking outside of yourself and at the bigger picture, I need to find tangible ways to share that with my class. On top of that, I want to cultivate a culture of cooperation and help within my classroom values (and hopefully within the school) that I am certain will add to the well-being and happiness of one and all.

Simply recognising and showing children that I, personally, value these qualities is a good start. It isn't enough, though. 'Actions speak louder than words' is one of my favourite sayings, and in my years of experience with children I truly believe that it is of paramount importance when it comes to teaching and passing messages: implicit teaching of values through our own actions is more valuable than any explicit teaching through words. Modelling the culture of cooperation I want to cultivate, being helpful and open myself, is my first step towards adding meaning to my pupils' days.

I am desperate to find some hands-on ways to infuse meaning into our school days. The theory is all there: I know this is important and that it will make a difference, but in practice it is hard. Religion can help people find meaning, but I teach at a secular school and besides, I want to find an equaliser: I have to create opportunities for finding meaning for all and then let the children discover their own meaningful activities for themselves.

Our very own pet?

I never thought a jar full of dirt would provide an answer to my quest. George is one of those kids you can't help but love: he is interested in everything, his heart is in the right place, yet his head is often in the clouds. I enjoy teaching him because he brings to me the unexpected; he has a wealth of general knowledge that challenges me and quirky interests which he shares regularly with me and the class. So I am not the least bit surprised when, one morning, he turns up with a jar full of dirt. The jar seems to attract an enormous amount of attention, but as I am busy I do not immediately engage in conversation.

During registration we go through our usual routine of sharing news. When George's turn comes I am very eager to find out about his jar of dirt and its relevance.

'Oh, it's not just dirt,' he beams at me, eyes twinkling. 'I have brought in some snails. From my garden,' he adds by way of explanation.

I freeze and wonder if I misheard. Or rather, I hope I have misheard. 'Why is the lid off?' I ask tentatively, though slowly I start realising that we are in trouble.

'I thought they needed to breathe!' he explains, sensibly.

I tiptoe towards the reading corner, wary of prematurely ending the life of any hapless gastropod who has made a bid to escape from his glass prison. I pick up the jar and peer into the mini-garden lovingly constructed by George. 'One, two, three, four,' I count with dread then look at him. 'How many did you have?'

'Hmm,' he seems unsure. 'Five? Or seven? I can't remember . . .'

Several children get up and start walking towards me. 'Freeze!' I shout and have to explain to them that the escapees could be anywhere. I pick one up from the edge of the table and look around for more.

Several minutes later, with half of my literacy lesson wasted hunting snails, we have located one more and are relatively certain that we have caught all of them. I sincerely hope so. At breaktime I sit at my desk, the snails all safely back in their jar, which by now has several small holes pierced into its lid. I wonder if there is any way I could use these little creatures to my advantage.

I have often read of schools which allow or even encourage classroom pets. The complications of what to do with a hamster over the long holidays, plus my mild aversion to keeping rodents as pets has, so far, stopped me buying into the idea. On the other hand I know that there are benefits to the responsibility of looking after a pet, and that looking after someone else is a good way to increase meaning in one's life. Research has shown that pet owners tend to be happier and healthier than their pet-free peers, they fare better on several well-being measures, from physical fitness to self-esteem. There are even studies that show that furry (and scaly?) friends can fulfil some of our social needs, while at the same time they do not compete with our human friends. I decide to keep the snails as classroom pets!

When I share the news with the kids, that we are to have our very own snail farm, they are delighted! They take responsibility right from the get-go: finding a suitable container for them to live in, instructions on how to look after them and designing a rota of care for them. I am pleased with the effect the snails have already had on the kids – they've stepped up to the challenge and worked hard, in order to give the snails a healthy and happy living environment.

We keep the snails for a few weeks and then, one rainy autumn day, we ceremoniously set them free with a wish that they may have a happy life out in the wild. They have added to our happiness over the last few weeks: the children simply enjoyed looking after them, and at the same time they added meaning and purpose to our days. Even pupils who are rarely motivated by academic work have been keen to come to school and put in some work to make the snails' lives better.

Now my challenge lies in finding a way to keep the momentum going. Snails are all well and good, and I'm pleased with how the children have reacted to the introduction of a set of pets into the classroom, but I keep thinking about meaning. Can I find some meaningful activities to enrich our school life on a deeper level? Over Christmas I read some research confirming that volunteer work improves several aspects of our well-being: happiness, life satisfaction, self-esteem, sense of control over life, physical health and mental health. But how can I get my pupils to volunteer when our days are so full already? These thoughts stay on my mind over the Christmas holidays and resurface again at the beginning of January, as we return to our busy school routines.

It is strange how, once you start thinking about a problem, the answers start coming to you thick and fast. In a way it is a trick of perception: I am simply looking at things with a different, renewed focus, but as I sit in the staff room discussing reading routines with my colleagues in Reception it comes to me . . .

61

Helping others

Right there, in our own school, lies a great opportunity to help someone else, the opportunity for my seven-year-old pupils to look beyond themselves and spend time assisting others. The Reception teacher and I agree on a date and time. When I tell my children that we are going to be reading stories to the younger kids the reaction is mixed: some are excited, some are not that impressed with the idea. I try not to lose heart and keep reminding myself that helping others is a way to happiness, so I prepare for our upcoming engagement with the youngest members of the school community.

The day comes and we join the little ones in the library. We put the children into pairs and threes and leave them to it. Much to our surprise the level of engagement is one of the highest we have ever seen. The older children seem to rise to the occasion and present a caring, warm side towards the little ones. Similarly, the little ones love being read to and seem to be very much at ease with my older pupils. It definitely looks like the activity is a success.

When questioned later it is clear my pupils have benefited in many small ways. Their self-esteem has received a boost and, yes, their happiness too: they feel like useful members of the community. They have done something to help someone else, adding meaning and satisfaction to their lives.

But why stop there? As a community, we are on a roll. So for my next challenge I want something a little more ambitious. I desperately want to help the kids create their own meaning; to find something relevant to them and take ownership of it.

Charity

Giving to charity can give a happiness boost. My first idea is to let the children find charities that they care about, and fundraise for them. But there are a couple of practical challenges here: how many different charities could we raise funds for, and how would we go about splitting the funds between them?

My colleague and I have another idea: we will link each of our learning topics to relevant charities. For example, when learning about rainforests, we will look at charities like the World Wildlife Fund and Rainforest Alliance. We will then let the kids decide on which charity to focus on, and come up with ways to raise funds. Similarly when we have water as our topic, we will look at different charities that help people have access to clean water. Suddenly, the children take charge. They have control of where the money goes and they start planning ways to raise it. They take full ownership of the process, planning and advertising for a bake sale, making posters to raise awareness for WaterAid and researching how their money will be spent by the charity. In a small way they lose themselves in the service of others – with all the associated benefits for themselves. What's more, I suddenly find myself feeling happier and more satisfied with life too! I knew there was a benefit to being a primary school teacher.

 ## At Home

A job for everyone

'We have to get Joe a job,' I tell my husband over breakfast one morning. He replies with a blank stare and keeps cutting up toast for our two year old. Our baby looks on.

'Like what? Our chimney could do with a good sweep,' he finally says, in a deadpan manner.

'OK, you know what I mean, not a proper job,' I continue. This time he looks a little relieved. 'I mean find him a way to contribute towards the running of the house, something he can do regularly and is age-appropriate.' I see my husband warming up to the idea. As a toddler, Joe loves helping out at home, though most of his help is, in reality, more of a hindrance. Still, I find a lot of value in it, and will let him be the one to unload the washing machine even if it takes him twenty minutes more than it would take me. For me, the concentration and look of satisfaction at the end is worth it.

But what I want for him is something he can take ownership of, something that can be his own responsibility, and something that isn't just about taking care of or tidying up his own possessions. I want it to be something that contributes to the whole family.

Looking after others

Trying to transfer some of the lessons that I have learnt from my teaching experience, I wonder if I can get Joe to help me with his baby brother. Oliver arrived when Joe was only eighteen months old, and can be a source of jealousy. I wonder if being more involved in his care would somehow take the edge off his negative feelings towards his brother? I really want the two boys to be close, and hope that involving my eldest in his baby brother's care can help, while at the same time reaffirming him as an active and helpful member of our little family.

In other cultures it is absolutely normal for older siblings to look after young ones, and in some countries children have close to full responsibility for their younger siblings. I don't want to burden my toddler with such a responsibility, but simply empower him by having him help his baby brother. Serving others heightens our sense of well-being: will it work for my two boys?

I start small, by asking Joe to fetch me a nappy or some baby wipes while I change Oliver. He is actively involved in the process, and I can see that it makes him happy. He is proud of himself, and visibly starts enjoying being a big brother. I, for my part, make sure I thank him profusely for being so helpful. A few days later I notice a change: Joe is actually looking out for his brother, without me asking him to. In fact, he finds his own job: in order to help his brother, he becomes the dummy monitor. Whenever Oliver's dummy comes out of his mouth, Joe alerts us to it and often tries to replace it, sometimes with success, sometimes with a little force. I make sure to thank him and try and explain to him that Oliver does not always want his dummy. But I can see how Joe is deriving satisfaction from helping his brother and I applaud his efforts.

Helping those weaker than us and giving to those in need are sources of happiness, but for a two year old it all needs to be put into a meaningful context. Taking my cue from my classroom experimentation, I encourage Joe to get involved in caring for our four dogs. He takes to the challenge with gusto, and, most of the time, my husband is grateful for the company. I am excited to think that this can be a long-term project. As Joe grows up, and later Oliver, they can increase their involvement with our animals in many ways: taking them for walks and grooming them could become part of the everyday routine of a primary-age child or a teenager – with added happiness benefits including being outdoors!

Thinking about ways to help older children and teenagers find meaning I ask around my circle of mum friends. Most report that chores are not in any way happiness-boosting in their families. I prod a little further. It seems that the sort of thing I had in mind for Joe, his way of giving back to the family, can be a source of argument and nagging for older children. I try and remind myself and my fellow mums that meaningful activities don't always feel like fun and they agree. On the other hand, the consensus is definitely that taking out the rubbish, although it is useful, is not seen as serving others or contributing to the greater good. I take note, and plan to leave these kind of chores well alone!

Cooking up a storm

What kind of chores work better for older kids? Ann, a mum of a young adult son and a teenage daughter, provides me with one answer. For her family, cooking is a way of giving back. Her kids, she tells me over homemade biscuits, started cooking for the whole family at the age of ten or eleven, and have done so regularly since. Even now that her son lives on his own, he regularly has them over for a meal, which he has shopped for and prepared himself. Cooking encompasses many happiness elements, and cooking for others can be a gesture of caring. Ann reassures me that, although they had their fair share of burnt food and slightly uncooked pasta in the first years that the children cooked for everyone, eventually it became a very sociable activity that everyone enjoyed. On top of that it taught her kids some useful, real-life skills that they could take away with them when the time came for them to move out. I certainly like the sound of that!

A virtuous cycle

I meet Katerina, single mum to a thirteen-year-old daughter, at a local charity bazaar. They are both behind a stall, selling cakes and coffee. First of all I am surprised, as Katerina certainly does not look old enough to have a thirteen year old. Then I am impressed. What a lovely way for mother and daughter to spend their Sunday morning. Finally, I am inspired! Spurred on by this and the research that suggests volunteering can boost our well-being I spring into action. All I need now is to find some suitable volunteering positions for children.

In certain school programmes (like the International Baccalaureate) volunteering is part of the curriculum. I speak to the programme director at one such school and she confides that, although at the beginning it is seen as a chore, quite a lot of the children end up enjoying it and continue to volunteer past their compulsory fifty hours. Anecdotally, it seems that children whose volunteer experience is highly social (for example, in a local old people's home rather than cleaning a beach) are more likely to continue after their required hours are completed.

The saying goes, however, that 'charity begins at home' and so I am still very keen to talk to a mum who finds a way to put that into practice. I observed Kelly, a mum of three, at home. I have gone for a toddler playdate, and immediately notice that the older children are very much involved with looking after their younger sibling.

'Culturally it's strange, I know,' she admits. 'But where I grew up, in rural Canada, being the fifth of eight children meant that I spent a lot of my childhood both being looked after and looking after my siblings.' She laughs and shows me a family photo. They do look very happy and wholesome. When I query about their 'happiness levels' she nods, then laughs. 'We were definitely happy! And we are still very, very close as siblings,' she adds, though I know that she has been away from home for the best part of a decade.

It seems there are many ways to help children find meaning, as well as letting them create their own meaning within our families and communities. Service towards others is a good way to enrich our lives, strengthen our connections and improve our well-being, while at the same time benefiting the wider community. A win-win situation, but one that is often overlooked, as we often forget to look at children as active citizens or imagine that they might have something to offer. This is one happiness habit that has a much wider scope – looking outside of ourselves can be deeply enriching and empowering.

The Magic Touch

'Touch has a memory.' *John Keats*

 ## The Idea

I cuddle my baby close to me and smell his hair. He instantly calms and looks up at me, a smile forming on his chubby face. At four months he is just learning to read my facial expressions, yet the most powerful of all communications between us is still that of touch and the easiest way to calm him down is to pick him up and hold him close to me.

We might not often think of it in these terms, but the skin is our body's largest organ. And as it is packed with nerve endings, it is one of the primary ways that we receive information about the outside world. Just one square inch in the palm of your hands has more than 72 feet of nerve endings! It should not come as a surprise, therefore, that touch is so important for our physical and mental health.

Babies are born into a world of touch. Cuddles, hugs and kisses are routine to the infant and they form a big part of his or her development. Touch is a fundamental piece of the puzzle for the emotional and sensory growth of babies.

But how can a simple hug or holding hands improve our mood and well-being? How do we keep touch in our daily routine as our children grow older? And how can we prioritise touch within our families and use it comfortably in our wider communities?

The Research

Imagine you're sitting in your local café watching two people you don't know. It's likely that you could guess quite a lot about their relationship based on how, and how often, they touch. It might also tell you quite a lot about what culture you live in: in one study from the 1960s, couples in cafés in Puerto Rico were seen to touch each other an average of three times per minute, while those in London averaged zero times per hour!

Fifty years on, whether we shake hands, hug or kiss when we meet someone remains just as influenced by the culture we live in. But using different types of touch to signal different kinds of relationships goes back a lot longer in our evolutionary history. In fact, a lot of what we know about the importance of human touch comes from looking at the behaviour of other species.

Our closest relatives, monkeys and apes, use touch in many of the same ways that we humans do. Many animals and birds groom themselves to remove dirt and parasites from their coat. But in the wild, primates spend a huge amount of time – up to 20 per cent of the day – grooming each other. This is usually a rhythmic combination of vigorous finger-thumb pinches that pluck out pieces of debris, mixed with gentler sweeps that provide a stroking sensation. And the main aim of all this grooming is not cleanliness, but social bonding. Grooming partnerships between two females can last for years and they spill over into other displays of loyalty. For example, the likelihood that a female gelada baboon will go to the rescue of another female who is attacked is directly related to the amount of time they have spent grooming one another.

In humans the effect of touch is so strong that even a barely-noticed touch can have a big effect on how we view another person. Well-controlled studies have shown that, for example, waitresses receive bigger tips after 'accidentally' touching a customer while returning their change, and students are more likely to volunteer answers if a teacher briefly touches their arm.

In children too, touching is a powerful driver of behaviour – just like in the young of other species. One very famous series of experiments looked at how important food was compared with physical contact in young monkeys who had been deprived of their mother. In these experiments, the baby monkeys had the choice of clinging to a warm, furry 'surrogate mother' or a cold wire one. They reliably chose the warm, furry one even when it provided no food, and when something frightening entered their cage they ran to the furry surrogate for protection – even if food came from the cold wire one.

We know that a lack of physical contact is bad for the young and, conversely, touch can have many positive effects on children's development and well-being. Touch therapies such as Reiki have been much less rigorously studied than conventional forms of medicine, so it can be hard to know how effective they really are. But the best evidence available at the moment suggests that touch therapies do cause a small but significant reduction in pain. In very young children, baby massage is often claimed to help with a wide range of problems. Like with therapeutic touch, this is considered a safe intervention with some potential, though more research is needed to better understand the potential benefits of massage in promoting things like physical growth and cognitive development.

From cats to monkeys to humans, being touched, stroked or groomed by another is often so pleasurable and relaxing that the recipient of the touch falls asleep. Touch releases a range of neurochemicals, including endorphins (which are similar in effect to opiates such as morphine) and neurohormones such as oxytocin. Sometimes called by tabloid newspapers the 'love hormone', oxytocin is indeed very important in social bonding. It is particularly strongly released in response to maternal and sexual stimulation, such as labour, breastfeeding and sexual activity. But even outside these intense stimulations, it is released in response to touches and stroking.

Usefully, synthetic oxytocin can be administered as a nasal spray, which makes its effects easy to manipulate and study in psychology experiments. These have shown that oxytocin affects many aspects of our social encounters, increasing pro-social behaviours such as trust, generosity, empathy and altruism, and decreasing fear, anxiety and stress reactions.

One effect of oxytocin is an increase in general feelings of well-being and, interestingly, it is released both when we receive a loving or comforting touch, and when we give one. For some kids, encouraging them to touch another being may be a good way to encourage their well-being. It doesn't even need to be another human: oxytocin is also released in us when we stroke a cat, and even when your pet dog gazes adoringly at you.

This is one reason why massage therapies are often encouraged in very ill children: as well as soothing the child, it also reduces stress and anxiety in the parent or other caregiver. Touch can lift the mood of two people at once: twice as much bang for your happiness buck!

PRACTISING THE HAPPINESS HABIT

 ## *At School*

'Can I play with your hair?' says Mara. We are in school, sitting on the carpet and cutting up what feels like hundreds of paper stars for our Christmas decorations, so I hesitate. Primary schools, it seems, are increasingly becoming touch-free spaces, what with fears of inappropriate touch between pupils and teachers, and the worry of rough play escalating into violence. As I tell Mara that she may not play with my hair, it dawns on me that touch is something so human, so deeply ingrained in our nature that it is difficult to banish it, especially from a place full of little people. On top of that, looking into the science it seems to be so beneficial that I wonder: should we really be making our school touch-free zones?

The need for touch is universal, but what touch is appropriate is deeply cultural. What is perfectly acceptable in one culture can be disturbingly familiar in another. Seeing two men greet each other by kissing is totally normal in Greece, while in Japan bowing is more the norm. Teaching in an international school, these differences started being highlighted all around me. One of the first things I noticed is just how physical many southern

European parents were with their children. Hugs and kisses at drop-off and pick-up time at school, holding hands with and carrying even older children, sitting on laps at an age where some British kids don't even want to be seen in public with their parents. What was more, I started noticing how tactile other adults were with kids too. Without apparent fear of being seen as inappropriate, adults would happily pat kids on the head, shake hands with, or pinch the cheeks of children they hardly knew. When I became a mum I found I had to consciously make myself relax as others patted my children on the back, pushed them on the swing or picked them up when they fell in the playground. It was the cultural norm and I would be doing my children a disservice by sheltering them from what was in fact harmless, socially appropriate touch.

I am not demanding we change cultural norms, or let strangers handle our kids. But I am determined to find culture-appropriate ways to introduce touch into our lives in class.

Many UK schools impose their own 'no-touch' policy: a blanket rule of no physical contact between teachers and pupils being a lot easier to enforce than a more nuanced rule. Interestingly, the rule is usually blatantly disregarded on a daily basis, especially in the early years classroom. How do you comfort a child, if you're not allowed to touch them? Every mum knows that sometimes words themselves are not enough and a cuddle can stop the tears a lot faster than abstract reasoning.

77

Shaking hands

At my current school rules are a lot more relaxed with regards to touching, and I soon decide that physical contact should be a part of the way I teach. I quickly find myself, consciously and automatically, incorporating touch into my daily routine with the class. One of the simplest yet effective ways I use is a personal handshake as children leave at the end of the day. Denoting mutual respect, but also full of warmth, it becomes my way of finishing the day on a high, while giving attention to each child individually. As children line up to say goodbye to me I relish the short time and undivided attention that I can give to each and every child. It soon happens that some children, unprompted, decide to opt for a hug instead, which I allow. The hugs, in fact, quickly spread and most of the children eventually show a preference towards a quick hug to the handshake at the end of the day.

As I start monitoring the way both I and the pupils use touch in the classroom I become very aware of the way it can convey many messages, not all of them desirable. Not only that but this kind of non-verbal communication can be stronger than words and so needs to be used carefully and thoughtfully. A pat on the head, for example, although often employed by teachers towards children in my school, can be seen as condescending by some. The same gesture can be a complete faux pas in some Asian cultures. At school, as an adult in a position of authority, it is clear that I have to be extremely careful.

A whole repertoire of non-verbal communication

Slowly I work on a repertoire of appropriate non-verbal gestures that involve touch to add to our days in class. One of the ways I manage this is by encouraging peer-to-peer interaction. High-fives became a valid way of expressing your admiration and support of someone's work, while pats on the back became a way of saying 'congratulations'. As a class we start developing our own non-verbal codes, all the while reaping the rewards of touch in our daily lives and developing a more close-knit community.

A gentle squeeze on the shoulder becomes a way of saying 'be quiet'. At first it starts with me, but then I think it could be an alternative to the finger-in-front-of-mouth gesture and employed by both me and the pupils themselves, so I encourage its use among my pupils too. Soon enough children are gently squeezing, or simply touching, their neighbour's shoulder in order to bring them back to the lesson.

Touch becomes increasingly normalised within our small community and is accepted by almost everyone. (It is worth noting here that one year I had a child in class who was on the autistic spectrum and found being touched and touching others very disturbing. We respected that and kept our distance, although by mid-year he was happy enough to exchange high-fives with his classmates.) As the year progresses I find that tactile expression enhances our connection to each other and helps lift our moods, and I start thinking more and more about our human need for touch. Watching children in the playground it is obvious that the younger ones spend a lot of their play relating to each other physically. Although occasionally physical play becomes rough, most of the time it remains strictly playful and appropriate. There is definitely a lesson for me here: children need this kind of play to explore boundaries of appropriate vs inappropriate, of rough vs soft. I find convincing arguments for it in DeBenedet and Cohen's book *The Art of Roughhousing: Good Old-Fashioned Horseplay and Why Every Kid Needs It*. In this interesting read, the authors argue that even rough play is all part of human contact, and that children should (and do) find the boundaries of what is appropriate by practising such physical games.

Touch and play

My challenge as a teacher, but not one for parents, is how to give opportunities for non-intrusive and appropriate sustained touch. The kind of touch that lowers blood pressure, reduces stress hormones and floods our bodies with feel-good chemicals. Aside from holding hands in line, which works well, I cannot think of any other ways.

One day, while we are on the carpet playing a grammar game which involves children sitting in a circle and building sentences by each adding a subject, verb, object in turn, it comes to me. It is a game I have been taught at a drama workshop a few years back and is called 'Pass the Squeeze'. It works like this: the children sit in a circle and hold hands. Then, starting from a given person the squeeze has to be passed around. When your right hand is gently squeezed, you have to pass on the squeeze to the person who is holding your left hand. Once kids get better at this, and believe me, they catch on quickly, we put in variations: playing with eyes closed, or even passing two squeezes around at the same time. A more advanced version which includes a double squeeze that reverses the direction of the game, is soon invented by the kids.

'Pass the Squeeze' becomes an instant hit and it is my solution to many problems, as it brings the kids to a quiet and fairly serene alertness quickly and easily. It also offers the much-needed benefits of sustained touch in an appropriate way to all the children at once. To my surprise, even my more touch-averse pupils enjoy 'Pass the Squeeze' and sometimes play it at break time.

 ## At Home

I start thinking about adding more tactile communication soon after my second son is born. With one young child it was easy: being his sole carer while my husband was at work meant that we spent a lot of the day physically playing, cuddling and kissing. I washed and combed his hair, we applied body lotion onto each other, we read books cuddled up on the sofa. When his brother arrives, things get a little more complicated. There is only one of me, and two of them. My time, attention and efforts at keeping both of them safe and happy during the day have to somehow be shared. With maximising tactile communication in mind, I start by taking stock.

I am a little surprised to find that while my older son seems to get quite enough one-on-one time with me, much of which is sharing skin to skin contact – physical play, pre-bed cuddles and bathtime caresses – my little one is being left out. It is easy to see why my eldest receives the lion's share of tactile affection: he voices his demands, he is proactive in coming to me for all his needs and, if nothing else, we already have a well-established routine. My little one, on the other hand, spends a lot of time sleeping and seemingly has simpler needs: eating, being changed and bathed are top of his agenda.

Once I have noticed the uneven split between my newborn and my toddler, I sit down with purpose. I have to somehow find the opportunity to give my precious newly arrived bundle a little more touchy-feely time. Theoretically, incorporating touch into one's day with an infant should be easier, but I am obviously missing some of the opportunities presented to me. My challenge is clear: how can I make the time to physically touch and cuddle my baby, when I am still spending most of my day running around after my toddler?

Baby-wearing

The answer comes from Lucy, a South African friend of mine, and it saves me in the early days of being a mum of two. I have noticed that my friend spends a lot of her day carrying her two-year-old daughter in a makeshift papoose. Sometimes at the front, and sometimes at the back, but either way most of the time her little one is on her, one way or another. In fact, when I ask Lucy to tell me about her sling she not only sings the praises of baby-wearing (a fancy name for carrying your child with the help of a sling, or carrier) but she shows me how to use a blanket to help me carry Oliver.

As I find fashioning a carrier out of a blanket a little too precarious for my precious newborn, I decide to invest in a proper carrier. That's when I learn that there are many different types, each with their pros and cons. A bit of research later (there is always research!) I settle on a soft, unstructured carrier called a mei-tai, one that allows me to wear either my baby or my toddler and which fits on either the front or back (the back being easier for activities such as walking, and safer for things like cooking). One of the factors in deciding on this particular sling is that I want no material between the baby and me, like some carriers have, so that we can both get the most benefit from the time we spend together. I find that a lot of the more expensive, structured carriers have a barrier between mum and baby – for me, defeating the whole point of carrying my baby.

I soon find that the little one loves being carried and nine times out of ten, he either falls asleep or calms right down when placed in the carrier. It seems that something in the warmth of my body, the sound of my heartbeat or simply being so close to me works wonders for calming him down when he cries (which was every evening like clockwork for the first three months). We love the mei-tai so much that we soon buy another one for our toddler, who, although older, also really enjoys being carried about by his dad. In fact the carrier becomes his safe place when we are out in busy shops, or at a museum. I can see that he often chooses to retire to his sling after being overstimulated or becoming simply too tired to deal with the world. There, against his daddy's back or chest, he often falls asleep, happily, while we get on with the rest of our day.

To my surprise my research into baby-wearing also uncovers some interesting facts, which confirm my own experience with carrying my newborn. It turns out that young babies who are carried cry up to 50 per cent less! In my case what that means is happy baby = happy mummy, with the added benefit of having my hands free to do chores, write or play with Joe! Needless to say, my youngest spends most of his first year in a mei-tai.

Baby (and toddler) massage

Another thing I am keen to try is baby massage. It seems to be all the rage and I have read a lot about its potential benefits. Many people report a calmer and happier baby – so I am determined to give it a go! Mind you, I am not going to take a course or go to classes, I am simply going to try and incorporate some soothing touch into our day. After some trial and error I finally find the ideal time for some loving strokes: nappy changing. It is something that I do several times a day anyway, and adding some lotion is easier than putting other time aside. I also find that, it being winter, there are few other opportunities in our day to have skin-on-skin contact.

As children come out of infancy and into toddlerhood and the preschool years, parents usually have to rethink their strategies for getting this all-important physical contact. Once more, experienced mums become my greatest source of information and inspiration. One of them is my own mum – a source I have discounted in the past, but who has a lot to share on this subject. Being Greek, she grew up in a house where touching and tactile affection were very much the norm. Finding out about my mum's childhood, a difficult but very happy time, brings into focus some of the practices from my own childhood too.

Touching rituals

In my mum's childhood home, there were three generations and five women under one roof, and physical contact seemed to have its own rituals. My mum and her sisters brushed and plaited each other's hair well into early adulthood, for as long as they shared a home. Other grooming behaviours were also very much the norm: cutting and painting nails and toenails, rubbing shoulders and feet after a hard day, even head massages. A lot of the activities we now, in our modern busy lives, pay someone else to do for us, were part of normal family life for my mum, her two sisters, her mother and grandmother, who all lived together when my mum was growing up.

I contemplate this as I sit at the hairdresser's, getting a complimentary head massage with my shampoo. It feels great, but here I am, having a stranger massage my head. In generations past this kind of intimate contact was reserved for family, increasing the feel-good factor for both participants, and also strengthening the bonds between family members. I am keen to introduce this into our family.

Maybe as a mum of young children I should be lowering my expectations. I chat to Gina, a mum of two older boys, one of whom is a teenager, the other aged nine. Gina is a young cool mum who is very much in touch with her growing boys. But does she get much physical contact in her days with them now that they are older?

She starts by telling me that the simple answer is 'no' but that it is a little more complicated than that. It seems to be the case that although the amount of tactile contact has diminished, she still manages to get affectionate touch from her boys. Greeting with a kiss and a hug is part of their family routine ('Yes, even for my teenager!' she confirms, laughing). I observe her with both her boys one day after school – they both kiss her on the cheek, and while Billy the youngest gives her a full-on hug, Harry, a cool teenager, side-hugs her.

Joining them in their after-school routine, I sit with them while they have a quick bowl of cereal, before they start their afternoon sports activities. She casually ruffles Billy's hair, and touches Harry's shoulder. It seems that she communicates with them with passing tactile gestures, which show affection and connection between them. I admire her ease, and the beautiful physical relationship she has maintained with her boys.

Later, while we chat over a glass of wine, she tells me just how important the boys' dad has been in maintaining the feel-good, magic touch in their family life.

'First of all, we are a very touchy-feely family,' she tells me. 'Even though my husband's German,' she laughs again. They certainly look like a happy family too. I ask her whether she thinks touch is correlated with happiness, in her experience, and within her family. She takes a sip and eats an olive, while contemplating the answer.

'It's a way of belonging,' she tells me at last. 'A way of saying: "We are a unit, a family!"' she continues. 'Jens and I make sure that the boys see us being physical: hugging and even kissing, in front of them.'

Then she said something that got me thinking: 'Jens still plays a lot with them, they get physical regularly, whether it is on the football field or after a run. Sport is a great excuse!'

Like lion cubs

That makes me think a bit more about the different roles that my husband and I have in the way my boys express themselves physically. My husband has a great way of normalising physical play with them, and fulfils a unique role in my sons' overall connection through touch. They fool around in a really playful, almost rough, way that reminds me of lion cubs playing with each other. Constantly defining and re-defining boundaries through play, he is teaching them daily what is acceptable and what isn't, while reaping the benefits of touch *and* play. Reframing our two different types of physical relationships I see that my husband's relationship is like lion and cub, while mine is more monkey to monkey, as we groom our way to physical connection. Two different but I think valid ways of increasing communication, comfort and well-being within our little family unit.

As I chat to other parents, I collect more anecdotes and it becomes obvious that touch is very much a family thing. The families who maintain physical connections seem to have a touch culture cultivated over many years. Those who remain tactile with their growing adolescents report hugs and kisses, but also massages and, wait for it . . . 'sitting on each other', as ways of staying close. Some report that the tactile, physical part of the relationship has become mostly the domain of the same-sex parent, as children get older. I can definitely see that happening to us: a good reason for both parents to stay closely involved as kids grow into adolescence and early adulthood. Overwhelmingly, though, I get a sense of the ease with which some families remain physically connected well into their children's adult years, maximising everyone's well-being.

Finding Flow

'Pleasure and action make the hours
seem short.' *Shakespeare*

 ### *The Idea*

Flow, put simply, is a state of being. We all know it. We have all
experienced it. We might not have a word for it, but we have all been
there. It is 'being in the zone', being totally absorbed in the task in
front of us, so much so that time and our surroundings disappear. In
other words, it is being in a state of optimal engagement. It happens
to me when I write (sometimes) or when I run in the mountains –
when my attention is so completely focused on the one thing that I
am doing that my mind has no more space for other thoughts and
time loses all meaning. It is a wonderful experience and one that can
add enormous amounts of happiness to our lives.

The question is: are children able to find flow and if so, what
should we be doing, as parents and teachers, to encourage them?

What sorts of activities provide this optimal engagement and how can we spot them? What are the elements of flow and how can we re-create them? And, finally, how do we help our children pro-actively choose flow-inducing activities?

The Research

Mihaly Csikszentmihalyi, who coined the term 'flow', had a big idea: that the way to increase happiness was not by thinking but by doing. Specifically, he thought that happiness arises from doing activities that have a higher likelihood of inducing flow. In his writing, he proposed many different characteristics of flow-inducing tasks. But as we are mostly interested in helping children to find flow at school and at home, we'll look at a couple that are most relevant to this situation.

One place to start is in understanding the relationship between a task's degree of challenge and a child's level of skill. How flow most often results from this balance is one of the most useful of Csikszentmihalyi's ideas. If you thought about it, you would probably predict that flow would occur when a task was neither too difficult nor too easy – that the perfect place for a child to experience flow would be where they were making good progress towards a goal, and where that goal was a reasonably challenging one. You'd be right.

Recent experiments have shown an added wrinkle, however: that the perfect balance between skill and challenge depends in part on how important the task really is to the person. For example, if a child is playing a video game and knows that ultimately, how well they do on the game doesn't really matter, then flow is most likely to occur at the more difficult stages of the game. Conversely, if the task is something where the outcome seems really important – perhaps a big homework project or an exam – then the child is more likely to experience flow at a lower level of difficulty.

There are a couple of useful implications of this. One is that we may want to encourage children to challenge themselves more during play-like activities where failure would not be disastrous, since this is more likely to be flow-inducing. Another is that, when trying to help children find flow, we need to take into account how much outside importance the child (and perhaps also the teacher or parent) is assigning to the task.

Of course, children differ in how seriously they take any particular task or its outcome. Are there also big differences between children in how and when they experience flow? Like any question that tries to objectively compare different people's internal feelings, this is a difficult question to answer. In fact, there is evidence that differences in the experience of flow are more related to the situation than to the individual. In one study, college students who were studying architecture were followed over fifteen weeks and prompted several times a day, at random intervals, about what they were doing and how they were feeling at that moment. It turned out that three quarters of the variation in flow that they experienced was related to the situation they were in at the time, and only one quarter seemed due to their (stable) personal characteristics.

So, while there are some inherent differences in people's tendency to experience flow, the good news is that the situations we put kids in and the tasks we encourage are likely to have a far bigger influence.

We can learn one other interesting thing from the architecture students study. Because the students were repeatedly asked about their experiences within a day, it was possible to track how the activities that they were doing earlier in the day affected their later mood, and vice versa. So, this and similar studies help answer the 'chicken and egg' question: does flow increase happiness, or are you more likely to experience flow when you are already happy? The good news is that, as Csikszentmihalyi predicted, good moods seem to follow after flow-inducing activities. So by setting up children to have more opportunities for flow during their day, we really are increasing the likelihood of a happy child.

PRACTISING THE HAPPINESS HABIT

 ## *At School*

I have been teaching for several years before somebody gives me Csikszentmihalyi's book *Flow: The Psychology of Optimal Experience*. I read it quickly and eagerly – and find that it chimes with so much of my experience with everyday activity.

I soon become acutely aware that a lot of the activities that we do in school have the potential for being enjoyable, in the sense that they are opportunities for optimal experience. Looking at the essential elements of flow, most school work – like solving a maths problem or writing an essay – encompasses these elements. They have a definite goal, they demand concentration, there is usually some feedback. And yet, it seems to me that in reality, very few pupils consistently experience flow in an everyday context in class. After all, if school were so full of flow-inducing activities and optimal experiences, children would love every minute of it. What can I do, as a teacher, to help children tap into the power of the optimal experience, to become and stay engaged and to truly find the enjoyment in the everyday life in school?

I start making modifications to both my teaching material and the way I present it. The first element that really strikes me as being directly under my control is the degree of challenge an activity holds. I think about this in my own life: I thoroughly enjoy reading and often find it flow-inducing. But if someone were to give me a book in Italian, or on advanced particle physics, chances are that the challenge to skill ratio would be too high for me to enjoy it. Similarly, I rarely enjoy reading children's picture books: the stories are too simple for me, and the element of challenge is missing altogether. (I would probably enjoy reading a simple children's book in Italian. A friend of mine who was trying to learn Spanish used to read children's books in the language and found the activity thoroughly engaging. The same books in English would not have held any challenge for her, but the sheer effort of deciphering a foreign language boosted her enjoyment.)

My quest for creating flow in the classroom is multifold. First, I want to give all pupils the opportunity to find flow within the academic activities of the class. Secondly, I want children to start recognising and seeking out flow for themselves in other activities. Finally, I hope children are able to actively choose experiences that provide this optimal engagement. Am I biting off a lot more than I can chew?

Flow in academic work

Ideally all work done in the classroom should be conducive to finding flow. In reality a very small percentage of children are able to find flow in most academic activities. Experienced teachers should be aiming to ensure that at least *some* activities fulfil the main criteria for encouraging flow. It is absolutely essential to remember that we cannot force a state of flow, we can only provide the right conditions for children to find it themselves, as well as teaching children to recognise it and seek it out.

Here are three of the main conditions that we, as teachers, have some control over. First of all, we can provide enough activities that are pitched right, that is activities that are differentiated and close to the right level for each child. I often find, in my class, that the best way to do that is to simply provide enough material that children find their own correct level. Much to my surprise, most of the time, my pupils can judge better than me the level of difficulty they can deal with. I am happy to see that by simply providing work that is differentiated three ways (an easy, intermediate and challenging level, for example) most kids can find something that provides the right ratio of challenge to their own skill level. In that way we avoid both the boredom that comes from too easy a task, and disengagement and loss of confidence from tasks that are just too challenging.

Another way to allow children to find their own appropriate level of challenge is to provide more open-ended activities. But these sorts of activities present another difficulty: that of giving adequate feedback to make the activity meaningful. Providing feedback or helping children to monitor themselves is a second important condition for flow that teachers can easily manage. Children don't always need praise, and when we are dealing with flow experiences, the experience itself and the resultant state should be its own reward. However, simple feedback, such as 'you're doing well' or 'you are on the right track' can help children monitor their progress and contribute to the optimal experience. I opt for minimal interruptions, a pat on the back or a thumbs-up as often enough to let the kids know they are doing OK!

Finally, the last condition: providing an environment free of distraction. By that I don't mean complete silence, but a space and a time where someone can work on their challenge without constantly being interrupted. I often let children pick their own place, during the day, so that they can find a spot on the carpet, or by the reading corner, where they feel happy to work.

I've done my best to help kids find flow through the academic work that we do every day. It becomes obvious to me quite quickly, though, that flow is something deeply personal and that all I can do is to create some of the conditions, and give children the opportunity to find their own personal flow activities.

Flow at play

I come across a paradox early on in my readings on flow and optimal experience: most of us experience more flow at work than we do during our leisure time. Work can be more like a game than some of the activities we choose during our downtime, especially if the latter are passive activities, like watching TV or reading non-challenging material.

This adds to the challenge of getting kids to actively seek out flow: I have to somehow help my pupils actively choose optimal experiences during play. But first I have to observe!

Unscheduled time is definitely at a premium in most classrooms. So the only time I can spare to experiment with flow-inducing activities is 'Golden Time'. Golden Time is quite commonly used in primary classrooms and often scheduled for a Friday afternoon. I want to have a good look at my pupils' Golden Time choices, observe the children during their chosen activities and then set up a more flow-friendly half-hour. Then I will step back and see what happens.

Usually, Golden Time involves me setting up several stations around the classroom and letting kids pick one of the activities on offer. Sometimes it is plasticine, Lego and drawing, sometimes it might be leftover art supplies, board games and access to the whiteboard. This time I want to try something different. I want to let the kids find their own activity to choose. This time my job is simply to observe.

This is what happens: a few of the kids, those who are generally able to occupy themselves, quickly find an activity, set it up and spend most of the half-hour completely engrossed. Sam spends his thirty minutes designing his own word search, while Nikolas decides to withdraw in the reading corner with a book. Anthony and Greg play chess. Two of the girls make a whole meal out of plasticine. But while some of the children hone in on their activity and spend a thoroughly enjoyable half-hour highly engaged, the rest of my pupils pick something up, then put it down and look for something else. They find it very hard to pick a suitable activity without guidance. I have to find a way to help them.

I spend the following week watching those pupils closely. I am trying to see how they choose to spend their time, what their strengths are, if there are activities that they naturally gravitate towards. But when it comes to Golden Time I do not tell them what to do. I write a list of possible activities up on the board and let the children choose freely. I offer some guidance, but do not make the choice for them. Then, when they have chosen an activity I offer a little more guidance. For example, when Fiona went to play with Lego I encouraged her to build a school: I nudge her towards a goal and towards something, within her chosen activity, that will give her immediate and constant feedback. She, to my surprise and satisfaction, remains engaged for the whole duration of Golden Time. At the end she spends quite a bit of time telling me what each part is and even asks me to take a picture of her school, to keep as a memento.

Although not everyone finds their optimal experience straight away, week after week children start finding out what they enjoy more, trying different things, learning to set their own goals and constructing their own optimal experiences. Not everyone manages to, but I am happy to see that *most* children learn to identify activities that give them that deep sense of enjoyment.

 ## At Home

Can babies be in flow? Recalling the sheer concentration that my son put into starting to crawl, the pure excitement at making each little move and the joy in his face when he would achieve his goal, I would have to say yes. A baby is acquiring skills constantly and is using those skills at the edge of his abilities, naturally finding his own optimal ratio of challenge and skill.

Toddlers also tend to be able to pitch their activity just right, and will then focus for a good amount of time on something, if we provide them with the opportunities. My son simply loved to build really high towers with his blocks and would find great enjoyment in adding just one more piece. He would become oblivious to his surroundings, to the point where I thought he was ignoring me when I called him for lunch. But when I observed him for a few seconds I could tell that 100 per cent of his attention was focused on this one self-set goal, with very clear feedback. It was obvious he was in flow.

Modelling

The cornerstone of parenting, and this case of optimal experience is no exception, is in modelling. Our children need to see us, their parents, deeply immersed in activities. They need to *observe* what it means to be thoroughly engaged and challenged.

The problem is, I am rarely able to concentrate 100 per cent on an activity while my children are around, so they never see me fully lose myself in any of my favourite pastimes. In the hope of increasing my modelling, I start leaving the door open when I work on my writing, or read a book while the children play in the garden. Soon enough my eldest will pick a book and come and read next to me, attentively looking at the pictures. He spends time scrutinising each and every one, occasionally pointing out a hidden bug or a flower he had not noticed before. Although I cannot say whether he is in flow, I am happy to show him I value reading and enjoy it a lot, and he seems to take that on board.

A writer friend of mine tells me that her eleven-year-old daughter has been watching her write for years, and recently she announced she wanted to start her own book. She has since started creating stories and spends hours writing on her laptop. It all sounds very encouraging!

Social flow

As we saw earlier, there is flow in most activities that involve challenge and feedback. It might come as a surprise to many that socialising is very much a flow activity. Clearly there are skills involved in good social engagement and, to introverts like myself, it can also require quite an effort. Socialising, especially when it is with more than one person, can have many of the elements of flow. It can be challenging, it can provide immediate feedback, we often get lost in it (how many times have you looked down at your watch after what felt like minutes with friends to realise several hours have actually passed?) and finally it often demands deep involvement from us. It might not have clear goals, but there are occasions, for example when we are part of a debate-style conversation, where that element too is present.

As parents we need to remember that the challenge of socialising is all the more present for most children and young adults who might still be building the extensive skill set needed for successful socialising.

Avoid over-scheduling

This is something I saw a lot of as a teacher! Of course we want to give our kids the best start in life and give them opportunities to find fulfilling activities. But sometimes children also need the freedom to control their own time, to choose their own activities and to experiment with doing different things. And that cannot happen when we have crammed their schedules full of structured activities: piano, golf, ballet and Mandarin!

Learning to ride a bike, playing a board game or even reading a book are all activities that have the potential to become flow-inducing and they happen during free time. You might think of reading as a relatively passive activity, but for young children just decoding the words can be extremely challenging, while a more skilful reader must read between the lines to decipher hidden meaning. The reader also paints pictures: what the characters look like, what seventeenth-century France smells and feels like. Finally, reading can tax our emotional intelligence: we empathise with the characters, make choices for them and anticipate the upcoming twists in the plot. In essence reading a book is not one skill, but involves a myriad of distinct skills that come into play as the reader becomes more proficient. So, reading for pleasure is certainly an activity that could promote flow at home.

Sports and games are often purposefully designed to be flow-inducing activities. They tend to give immediate feedback, have a clear goal and most of us, if the challenge level is right, lose ourselves in the game. I remember, as a child, playing board games for hours at home with my brothers – lost in our own (fairly competitive) world.

I could give lots of examples of opportunities for flow, but ultimately we need to keep in mind that optimal experience is something deeply personal. Knowing our kids, *really* knowing them and what makes them tick, can help us guide them in making the right choices on how to spend their time. Even better, when we help kids know themselves, then they can seek out the sorts of activities that will fulfil them. We need to remember that one person's enjoyment is another person's nightmare. My brother used to really enjoy and get lost in solving algebra problems. For him they ticked all the boxes: they were just the right difficulty level, offered a challenge, they had a very obvious end, a solution and he would get lost in them for hours. But give the same activity to me and I would shudder at the thought of spending even five minutes looking at it: I lacked the mastery and therefore the inclination to even begin solving one of them.

As parents, all we can do is give our children the opportunity to be involved in flow-inducing activities and help them recognise flow when they experience it. In that way our children can learn to choose activities that are not merely pleasant, but actively enjoyable, optimal experiences! We can also show them, through our own actions, that we value such optimal experiences: children who see their parents involved in enjoyable, fulfilling work – be it a hobby or employment – will learn to value such enjoyment. Undertaking such activities together can be a source of enjoyment, as well as bonding. A game of tennis with your teenager, or a game of chess with your eight year old can be a great source of flow for both of you. Solving a puzzle or working on a jigsaw, learning a new skill like dancing or cookery, all of these activities can bring us together as a family.

 ## Tech it up

While there are reasons to limit the amount of time kids spend staring at screens, video games, especially world-building games like Minecraft, can provide a lot of the elements of flow. Make them a little more social by playing 'doubles' or having a tournament.

Happy Choices

'Happiness resides not in possessions, and not in gold, happiness dwells in the soul.' *Democritus*

 The Idea

Pause for a moment. Think of the things that give you the most happiness in life. Chances are what you have in your mind right now are not possessions, but people, relationships and experiences. And although that's no secret, many of us still live our lives, and bring our kids up, in ways that emphasise material goods over the things that really make us happy.

I imagine I am not alone in this, that every new parent is surprised by just how much 'stuff' seems to come along with a baby. Clothes, cribs, car seats, buggies: even before I became a mum I was overwhelmed with the amount of consumer choices I had to make for my future offspring. After becoming a parent these choices only increased, and started permeating every inch of my life. Some parenting decisions (organic or not, baby-led weaning or mush, sleep training or co-sleeping) caused me a lot of sleepless nights. I longed for some simplicity in my life, yet paradoxically, I fiercely defended my ability to choose. I felt that the more choices I had the better off I was. But was that true?

Autonomy – the ability to have control over our life and choices – is an important part of happiness. But there is a catch: for ourselves, and our kids, more choice does not necessarily mean more happiness. Dealing with children both at school and at home I have often found myself struggling with competing desires: to provide my kids with everything they want, but not drown under a layer of plastic toys; to let them make choices, but nudge them towards the right ones; to motivate them to behave well, without bribing them.

The questions mounted: should I be using material rewards or not? Just how many toys do they need? How can I help my kids to make choices they are happy with, fostering their autonomy without overwhelming them with decisions?

The Research

There may be people out there who can say that, in all honesty, they have never resorted to bribing a child with a new toy, with sweets at the supermarket checkout or with access to a forbidden gadget like Daddy's phone. I'm not sure I know any of them. In moments of desperation, we usually assume that the thing most likely to stop the tantrum, or enforce good behaviour is, well, a thing. In calmer moments we may try and instil a less instant and materialistic reward system, perhaps using a weekly star or sticker chart to earn access to special privileges.

This process is, after all, how the adult world works: if I work hard and succeed in my job I am rewarded with a salary – and perhaps even a bonus. But mostly what makes us happy at work isn't knowledge that money is accruing in the bank. It's working in a team, designing new projects, making good on our responsibilities, and being recognised for a job well done. Would you be happier being paid a lot more money to do something very boring? Probably not.

It turns out that children are not so different. In fact, a host of psychological studies show that 'bribing' children with tangible rewards can actually make the thing that is being rewarded seem less appealing. In particular, offering to reward children for doing something that they already find interesting causes their motivation to actually go down. And offering rewards for activities that are not interesting doesn't improve their motivation to do them, either.

So what does research suggest is the most effective way to get kids to do some of the boring but necessary tasks in life? Well, like adults, kids prefer to do tasks when they understand the purpose of the task: 'because I said so' isn't the best motivator. Kids also, like adults, very much value their autonomy, so they are much more likely to be happy doing something if they have had a choice in whether or not to do it. In one study, children were given boring tasks along with explanations that varied in how much the purpose of the task was explained, and how much choice the child was told he or she had over doing it. Kids rated short but boring tasks as more enjoyable if they were given instructions that emphasised that taking part was their choice. (This is an example of cognitive dissonance, the tendency we all have to rewrite our explanations for our actions so that they make more sense.)

That children find choice rewarding is true both at home and in the classroom. In a large study in Israeli schools, researchers looked at links between how much children liked school and differences between teachers in the extent to which they encouraged or discouraged autonomy. They found that even young schoolchildren could easily identify behaviours which encouraged autonomy, such as allowing criticism, and behaviours that discouraged it, such as enforcing meaningless rules. Being less engaged with school was strongly associated with a lack of autonomy, for example in those children whose teachers repressed criticism in the classroom.

Interestingly, it's not only kids who find schoolwork difficult, or who have a hard time obeying the rules, that find a lack of autonomy at school so off-putting. Even among high-achieving children, those who are more involved with school, who enjoy it more and are more likely to persist with difficult tasks, tend to give many more autonomous explanations for their behaviour ('I do my homework . . . because I want to understand the subject') than those who are less involved and get less enjoyment ('I do my homework . . . so I won't get in trouble').

So giving children choice, rather than things, is probably not only a more effective reward in the short term, but it also encourages an autonomous way of thinking that should help them in the longer term too.

PRACTISING THE HAPPINESS HABIT

 At School

Moving from material rewards to fostering autonomy

Pupil-of-the-week awards, gold stars, stickers and other rewards – what teacher (and parent) has not used these? They seem to be part of the basic currency of learning, the attempt to motivate and engage our pupils. And yet, looking at the research, it seems that there are better ways. Not only that, but in some ways they hinder motivation and engagement. I am interested to see how my pupils will respond to the removal of such external motivators. I'm in for a bit of a surprise! It is a few months into the school year when I inform my pupils, apologetically, that there are no more stickers for a few days. The response I get is a lot stronger than I expected. Many pupils are upset, some even voice their feelings, by telling me something along the lines of 'no stickers, no work'. I am gobsmacked by the level of reliance on these props. I decide that I probably need to go cold-turkey and remove such external rewards from my arsenal of tricks as a teacher. However, in a bid to foster independence and autonomy, something that the research shows can make children happier, I decide to replace material rewards with choices. For example, kids could pick their own activities, or, as mentioned in the chapter on Singing, can 'pick the tune' that we sing that week, make choices about the materials they read or simply choose who to sit with.

I go to talk to Mark, a teacher I know, who doesn't use stickers or gold stars. One of the best-loved teachers in his school, he seems to do the job by motivating his pupils in others ways.

'I try and teach them the joy of creating, or learning something new,' he tells me. His classroom is an exciting place. It is messier than most in the school, but every corner seems to have a different project going on. His pupils seem engaged and happy. And they absolutely love their teacher!

'It wasn't so much a conscious decision,' he continues, 'but I found that I constantly forgot the stickers and needed to be reminded of the stars. Eventually I embraced it as a new philosophy and it has done my pupils no harm! They have a choice of activity as a reward,' he tells me, pointing around at the various 'stations' in every corner of his room. All I see in front of me are motivated pupils, happily getting on with their work. Mark agrees with that. 'They certainly don't miss their gold stars!' he tells me emphatically.

My pupils too, it seems, get used to trading their gold stars for the privilege of choice. One of the things they like the most is having a choice of reading materials and I reward them with free rein over the class library books. Although this ability to choose seems a great motivator, a few weeks into it, we run into a problem.

A nudge towards happy choices

I can see Marina is getting frustrated. She has become immobilised by choice and is unable to make a decision. We're coming to the end of our allocated library time and she is no closer to choosing a book than thirty minutes ago. A brief chat with her is enough for me to understand why. Marina is a 'maximiser', she wants to be sure she is picking the absolutely best option, and she is simply paralysed by the hundreds of choices she has. This is frustrating, and, according to research, even after Marina manages to choose she is more likely to be unsatisfied with her choice. Anna on the other hand is a 'satisficer', she is happy with any book that is, in her mind, good enough. She spent about five minutes looking for a book and she has been sitting and reading happily since.

I can definitely see the difference between Anna and Marina – but I wonder if there is something I can do to help them be happier when choosing and happier with their choices. In his very successful book *The Paradox of Choice: Why More is Less*, psychologist Barry Schwartz analyses how we make choices and the way to being happier with the choices we make. It turns out that it all comes down to learning, and teaching kids, that sometimes you don't need 'perfect', sometimes all you are after is 'good enough'. I know, in a way this goes completely against a culture that chases and rewards perfection. However, I am pretty certain of this: if we all learnt to settle for good enough a bit more, we would all be a bit happier. This concept extends to most of the choices that we make on a daily basis.

On a more practical level I want my pupils to be able to make decisions easily and with minimal dissatisfaction. I am well aware of the children who get paralysed by choice, even simple ones like which pencil to write with, which book to choose or what game to play during playtime.

I look to the literature for ideas. Much to my surprise what I find there is a whole concept, Choice Architecture, that is there to guide me. After reading a little I understand what the problem is: choice overload. Having too much choice paralyses some of my pupils and they are simply unable to choose. I need to find ways to help them optimise their choice.

Optimising choice by limiting options

I find that there are several things that I can do to help my pupils in their choices. First, I can simply reduce the amount of choice they have. I can do that by asking them to choose amongst a subset of books, for example asking them to only choose non-fiction books this week, or only a certain writer's books the next. I use this technique in more and more aspects of school. By limiting, but not eliminating, choice I can see children are quicker to make a decision, and usually seem happier with the decision that they make.

Making a default choice available

Another tactic I start employing is making a default choice. For example, I assign each student a book per week. They have the option of looking for another one if they wish, giving them autonomy, but I am surprised by the fact that over half of my pupils prefer to take this book, rather than look and make their own choice. Choosing by default is a common trick used by policy makers to 'nudge' us into making difficult decisions, like savings and pension plans. I am amazed at how liberating some kids find this and I am definitely pleased with the results. It seems that they now spend a lot more time enjoying their books, rather than looking for the ever-elusive perfect choice.

 At Home

Drowning in toys

According to Statisa.com, in the UK, we spend on average $438 (£309) on toys for every child, every year. This tops the table of consumer spending on toys around the globe, but the US and France follow with a spend of over $300 (£211) a year per child. The annual toy market in the UK is worth almost $5 billion (£3.5 billion). On the one hand it is astounding to hear such numbers, on the other I am not so surprised.

Before we became parents, my husband and I had thought about this long and hard. We were adamant that we wanted very few toys, ideally wooden, and definitely no battery operated ones! Of course, this resolution went out the window pretty soon after our son joined us. Although we stuck to our guns and bought nothing, toys came streaming in, presents from friends and family and generous donations from parents whose kids had outgrown their baby toys. It soon became difficult to control this flood of plastic and batteries, which threatened to not only take over his room, but also started spilling over into our lounge, the garden, the bathroom, with toys for the bath and occasionally even the kitchen.

With the arrival of our second child, I feel inundated. Despite the fact that we always ask for books or toiletries as presents, there somehow seems to be an endless stream of new toys into our lives. Toys that the kids seem to play with for only a little while, then put away and forget about. In a mostly futile attempt to stem this continuous influx, I cunningly remove and give away some toys every month: interestingly the boys don't seem to miss them or ask after most of them.

What I notice is this: the more toys my eldest has out, the less he plays. He flits between this and that, not concentrating on anything, not really settling down to play with anything. Then he goes into the box and gets more toys, scatters them about and continues to . . . not play with them. He seems unhappy with each and every choice, like he feels there is always another, better, toy in the box. Eventually worn out, he often turns to me for entertainment. I am sure there is another way.

I want my child to grow up to be able to pick something and stick with it and to be happy with his choice. But as with everything I probably need to nudge him towards the right direction.

The toy cupboard is our first solution. We keep a selected number of toys in the cupboard, accessible by us, and he asks for whatever toy he wants to play with. He seems to go through phases of choosing one particular toy over everything else, and he really, truly plays with it. He concentrates on his toy, creates stories and worlds around this one item. When he is finished it goes back in the cupboard, and if he wants another toy, the first toy usually goes back (apart from the rare occasions where his storymaking depends on the combining of a couple toys together).

This keeps him a lot happier, more engaged. He misses his toys, but in a good way, and is happy to see something he has not played with in a while come out of the cupboard. He enjoys choosing a different toy every day, or sometimes simply the same toy again and again. He is empowered by the act of choosing but rarely finds it hard to choose: he knows what he wants to play with and he plays with each toy for longer and in imaginative ways. Mission accomplished.

The regular toy purge

Taking note of the research from the University of British Columbia that suggests that children, even those under the age of two, are made happier by giving to others, I decide that it is time to give away! There will hopefully be two benefits to this: the act of giving itself will make us happier, and having less clutter around the house and fewer toys to choose from will also play its positive role in my children's well-being at home.

We pick the last Sunday of each month to choose toys to give away. But I want to make this special, so we don't just pick the toys, shove them in bags and simply throw them out, in a glorified 'binning'. I want to give the boys a sense of 'gifting' these toys. I want them to think a little bit about the joy these toys will bring to someone else, I want them to be thoughtful of who might get these, and I want them to prepare the toys and truly make them into a gift. Joe insists on wrapping paper, which at first I find onerous, but then I think is brilliant!

We get into the routine of truly thinking what might make others happy. In the beginning I feel a little hesitant, guilty even, for making such demands on my young sons. But then I notice that my eldest, at least, actually enjoys the process. He is happy to give away some of the toys he does not play with much, provided he chooses which ones and we wrap them up properly.

I'm in for a pleasant surprise when we have our regular playdate too. Usually the boys play alongside each other, vaguely aware of each other's presence, but more interested in the toys than in playing together. It takes a few weeks of having a limited choice of toys, but this time, when Thomas comes to play I only put out one toy: Joe's tool set. To my surprise (and that of Thomas's mum) the boys sit together and pretend to fix first a chair, then what I presume is an imaginary car. They play for a good while before building a fortress with the sofa cushions and pretending to be knights (I think). They hide from each other and squeals of delight reach us, as we sit in the kitchen and watch them have fun. The boys have gone from toy-centric play, to child-centric play in a few short weeks.

A birthday without toys

Nico is turning five. He is having a party at a local playground and his mum has asked us for no presents. Instead, she has informed us that we can make a donation to a children's charity. I love the idea and explain it to my eldest as we prepare for the party. When we get there I help him put some money in an envelope, write a note together, which he proudly 'signs' and we discuss what the money we are donating might buy for the children at the receiving end. Joe seems very happy about it all, but I want to know how Nico is taking it, so I call his mum a few days later.

'It has always been this way for him,' she explains to me. 'We have done it right from the beginning, so he knows that his birthday is not so much a day when he gets presents from everyone, but the day when he gives something special to children who are not as fortunate as we are!'

I ask her about how their friends and family have taken it and she laughs. 'Well, it certainly took the grandparents several years to stop buying him stuff, but now most of our close friends and all of our family are on the same page. Grandma has established a different tradition with him, actually, and she usually takes him out for a treat: an ice cream, a waffle or a theatre trip.'

All that sounds wonderful, but I want to talk to Nico too. I ask him if he minds about the toys and he explains to me that he has enough already. I ask him what he likes to play with best and he tells me he has an 'awesome trainset with batteries' and some 'proper Lego'.

Experiences over stuff

'You will never guess what Sonja wants for Christmas!' Milena tells me. She continues to explain that her thirteen year old has asked for a hiking trip!

'For years we have opted for experiences instead of things: one year we went go-karting, another we booked a horse riding weekend. We have done this since they were little. This year she wants to travel!'

Experiential presents are such a great idea. I hear of several families around us who practise this, especially since the financial crisis hit Greece.

'We make a special day, and he gets to choose his own treat,' says Joanna, mum of eleven-year-old Alex. 'He chooses a cinema trip, a bowling evening or ice-skating. We usually schedule it for after Christmas, we get time to catch up and for the last few years he gets to pick a couple of his friends to join us.' I ask her how he deals with having free choice, and she explains that she always gives him 'ideas' to choose from. 'I never let him choose freely, as it were. There are always options, usually about three to four, things I know we can afford,' she explains to me.

While we chat I remember having read about the idea of creating 'the gift of time' with vouchers that can be redeemed throughout the year. Ideas might include a trip to the zoo together, baking muffins, an extra-long bedtime story, a new coffee shop to visit together, a playdate with some of his favourite friends. We both love the concept of the vouchers and vow to try it come next Christmas day!

The Great Outdoors

'Just living is not enough . . . one must have sunshine, freedom, and a little flower.' *Hans Christian Andersen*

 ## The Idea

Even on a cloudy day, venturing out seems to lift my mood. The fresh air, nature or even just being away from the four walls of an office or a house can turn a day around. Yet, increasingly we, and our kids, tend to spend more and more of our scheduled time inside: at work or school, but also during our leisure time, staring at screens instead of smelling flowers, and lounging about instead of baking mud pies.

In his bestselling book *Last Child in the Woods*, Richard Louv coined the term 'nature-deficit disorder'. While he was not implying that this is a real medical condition, he was highlighting a key issue in modern lives, and suggesting that reconnecting with nature can make us physically and mentally healthier, and improve our well-being. I agree with him wholeheartedly. The more time we spend outside the more balanced we seem to become. The stresses of everyday life appear more manageable under open skies, and I cannot think of a better way to spend leisure time than in nature.

So my challenge is clear: I need to build more outside time around my kids' busy schedule. But how much nature do we really need in order to reap the benefits of being outdoors? And how is it possible to make going outdoors a positive habit all through the year?

The Research

Stuck indoors with kids who are bursting with energy on a rainy day, it may seem blindingly obvious that time outdoors equals happier kids. In fact there are many different benefits to children of spending more time outdoors, aside from just being a great opportunity for everyone to let off steam.

First of all, let's deal with physical activity. Current UK guidance is that children under five should spent at least three hours a day being physically active, and school-age children and teenagers at least one hour each day. Being active helps children to maintain a healthy body, combating the worrying rise in childhood obesity, and helps the development of bones and muscles, balance and motor control. To build this habit, starting early really matters, because how active children are in their early years predicts how active they will be throughout their childhood and into adult life.

So being active is important to kids' health and well-being, and research has shown that spending more time outdoors is the easiest way to increase young children's activity levels. The more time kids spend outdoors, the more active they tend to be. Interventions such as increasing the amount of outdoor space and outdoor play equipment available to children are good for increasing activity in school-age children. Importantly, exercising outdoors has also been shown to be more relaxing, stress-relieving and mood-boosting than the same activity completed indoors, as well as more enjoyable. This matters because in children, as in adults, enjoying an activity increases the chances that it will be repeated, eventually becoming a lifelong habit.

Another way that being outside directly impacts well-being is through vitamin D production. Responsible parents and teachers often worry about exposing children to sunshine because of the risk of skin cancer, especially in countries where children are not genetically adapted to deal with sun exposure through darker skins. But the widespread use of high-factor sunscreen, coupled with a lifestyle where children spend more time indoors than they historically would, has resulted in many children (and indeed adults) being deficient in vitamin D, which is primarily sourced through the effect of sunlight on skin. Vitamin D is an essential component for healthy bone growth, and children and teenagers who lack vitamin D may have an increased risk for conditions ranging from obesity and metabolic disorders to infections and allergies. Vitamin D is also very necessary for healthy brain development, and it has been suggested that a lack of vitamin D increases risk for brain disorders such as depression, schizophrenia and multiple sclerosis.

Daylight also plays a powerful role in regulating circadian rhythm, our internal body clock that controls things like metabolism, alertness and mood throughout the day. When our circadian rhythm is unsettled, for example by jetlag, or working a nightshift, many aspects of our mental well-being suffer. During the winter months in particular, a lack of daylight exposure in some people seems to lead to seasonal affective disorder (SAD, often known as 'winter blues' or 'winter depression'). Increasing exposure to daylight – through natural or artificial means – is an effective treatment for SAD in adults and is now being tried too in younger people. It is thought that this light therapy works in part by providing stronger cues to reset and maintain the circadian rhythm. Getting out in daylight more may also help non-depressed teenagers, who seem to have a sleep–wake cycle that is biologically less well-regulated than that of adults.

So being more active and being outdoors during the day are both likely to improve our children's well-being. There is a third line of research that we should also consider, and that is the effect of the type of environment that they go out into.

People who feel more connected to nature show higher levels of happiness, vitality and life satisfaction. In children, access to natural environments seems to considerably affect mental well-being and development. For example, low-income inner-city children who move to greener environments show a reduction in ADHD-like behaviours. Among rural children, access to green space increases their resilience to life stresses such as house moves, school problems or conflict with other children.

How does nature have this effect? One theory is that when we're in natural environments our attention is constantly captured by interesting but relatively stress-free stimuli – views, sunsets or just the pattern of leaves on a tree. In contrast, in urban environments, we need to remain more aware of the 'bigger picture' – for example, to avoid getting hit by a car or bumping into someone on the street. In the city, when our attention is captured by something it's likely to require more urgent action, such as the sound of a vehicle approaching. This difference in demands on attention is one reason we find being in nature more relaxing and restorative than being in a busy city. Experiments have shown that being in a natural environment, or even just looking at pictures of nature, can temporarily improve our ability to appropriately direct our attention. It is likely that even a brief period of 'nature time' can in this way be a helpful boost to concentration for children, as well as those caring for them.

PRACTISING THE HAPPINESS HABIT

 At School

The ideal: forest schools

Forest schools have become more widespread in much of northern Europe. Outdoor education, the freedom to interact with nature and a school outside the confines of four walls is an idea that inspires. I find an article on Danish forest schools and devour it. I read about the opportunities and the challenges of teaching children in vast outdoor spaces and I feel like I too have discovered something special. The more I read about it the more I love the idea of forest kindergartens. I vow to try and incorporate some of the practices into my school day. Then I realise that it's going to be quite a challenge. First, because I teach in Greece which, culturally, does not associate education with the outdoors. They might like eating and drinking al fresco and many of them could not possibly envisage living in a house or flat without even the smallest outdoor space, but when it comes to education it all needs to happen in a classroom.

Secondly, Greece is blessed with wonderful weather. There are four distinct seasons and the temperatures are within comfortable range most of the time, with the notable exception of some very hot summer months. You might think that good weather would make people more likely to go out, but in reality if the weather is not perfectly accommodating the Greeks will not venture out. I'm guessing the reason is, if the weather is not great today, it is very likely that by tomorrow it will be fine. So why go out today, in the rain, when you can wait until tomorrow and walk in sunshine?

I read about '*friluftsliv*' or life in the open air, a very Scandinavian concept and realise that that's exactly what I need: to bring the very spirit of '*friluftsliv*' into my classroom. So I start as close to home as I can: an interview with some of the Scandinavian parents at the school, as well as some of my own Swedish, Finnish, Danish and Norwegian mummy friends. Essentially I want to know how they incorporate this love of nature in everyday life and hopefully gain some insights that I can use with my class.

After several interviews, a lot of advice and inspiration, I distil the major points and start making more concrete plans. Ideally we would be out there chopping wood and learning directly from the natural world. We would be building shelters, jumping into puddles and designing our very own bridges to cross streams. But this strikes me as impossible given both our location and cultural background, and so I vow to find other ways to include more of nature and the outdoors into our days.

The reality: introducing the micro-break

My friend Lilja reminisces about her childhood. She has spent the last hour telling me about growing up in Oulu. I found it hard to grasp that one can have an outdoor lifestyle living just 100 miles from the Arctic Circle. Later on, when I find out that the average annual temperature in Oulu is 2.7°C, I am even more impressed. As Lilja tells me about her school years, it sounds like nature was a big part of growing up. However, I'm most interested to hear about the school day structure: this is potentially something that I can incorporate into my teaching day too.

She tells me how Finnish schools tend to have a short break during every teaching hour: after every forty-five minutes of learning inside, there is a break of fifteen minutes, which often takes place outside. Although pupils are not forced to spend their break actively the kids still benefit from being outside. Fresh air, sunshine when available and some contact with nature in the school's surroundings, can certainly help increase feelings of well-being.

Although I don't have fifteen minutes to spare in every hour of teaching, my class is close enough to the playground that a quick run-around is not impossible. I start small, adding a little run-around every time we have a change of location. Every time I pick them up from the music room, we go back to class via the playground. The same happens after our library session or computing lesson. I want to see whether the short outdoor break will have any effect on the kids. Part of me is worried that they will be distracted and that it will be difficult to get them back to work, but another part is definitely excited by the possibility. It is also a good opportunity for me to stretch my legs! To gain the most from our short break I suspect that a quick burst of activity might be most beneficial. I don't have to tell the children that, though, they are happy enough to run around even if it is only for two minutes. That is exactly the amount of time I have to spare. One minute to go outside, two minutes to have a quick run-around.

And it seems to work. Contrary to my fears, the children work harder in between breaks and seem to be in a better mood when we come back in. They enjoy our quick run-around, and I commit to adding more of them to our days. I still shy away from taking the kids outside if the weather is not good, but thankfully we are in Greece and the weather is good most of the time.

Taking the classroom outdoors

The next step in my quest for more time in nature is to take some of my teaching out into the fresh air. I agonise over it a lot, and, although I want a 'forest school' the closest I can get is using some of the picnic benches outside for work that would otherwise take place in the classroom. It is not really in the spirit of forest school at all: we are not immersing ourselves in nature and we are certainly not utilising the great resources around us in order to learn. All I am doing is taking the inside, outside. I am not entirely satisfied with this, but I struggle to find a way to add a regular outdoor adventure to our daily routine. We do go outside, especially when there is some sort of curricular link. For example, when learning about the water cycle, we use the playground to make puddles of water, then watch and record as the water evaporates in the midday sun. Similar projects happen all around me: other teachers are also taking their classes outside to design shelters, to look at the local stream, to talk about habitats, to look for minibeasts. But is that enough? And how do I find nature within our semi-urban environment?

Urban nature

Not every school has ready access to nature, or even some green space. One of the schools I worked at in England was situated right next to the village green, and had direct access to the river. We did take some advantage of the location: our PE lessons were always on the green and we occasionally went out there for breaks or a run-around. But had I known then what I know now I would perhaps have made use of our natural surroundings more often.

Most of us think of nature as something far away and untouched by humans. But in reality nature exists all around us. It lives in our cities, it coexists with our motorways and it is certainly found in our homes too. Even the most urban of landscapes has some kind of natural aspect to it and I am determined to find it!

It is the beginning of autumn, the first rains have come and there is a certain scent in the air. I am determined to show kids that nature is all around us, even for those of us who live in the centre of town, so I decide to do a 'season watch'. Each child has to take a picture of the landscape outside her house, and present it to the class with a few sentences on what she can hear (birds chirping, the rustling of leaves or simply the wind whistling) and what she can smell (freshly cut grass, flowers the smell of rain on dry tarmac). We will repeat the exercise at the beginning of each season, looking for ways that our urban landscape changes throughout the year. All I want to achieve with this exercise is to make us all a little more aware of the biodiversity of our urban locales and bring a little more awareness of the natural elements that exist all around us, even in our cities.

Soon kids come to me with reports on different animals they have seen, on the nesting habits of pigeons in the centre, on the leaves that have been falling from the trees (which some kids had not even noticed before). I am pleased to see that we are all noticing the beauty of urban nature.

One of my pupils, Ariane, decides to make a birdfeeder to place on her third floor apartment balcony and that gives me an idea too: we make some peanut butter feeders and place them in our playground just as winter is approaching. The birds are certainly shy when the kids are out, but every once in a while, during our lessons, we glance outside to see all sorts of little feathered creatures enjoying a treat!

Bringing the outdoors in

For help in this project, I am lucky to have help from a colleague who is a trained botanist. She has a little 'nature corner' in her room and has been encouraging me to start my own for ages. Inspired by research suggesting that indoor plants can boost attention and contribute to higher levels of well-being, I (somewhat reluctantly) agree to bring some plants into my classroom too. The kids agree to help me look after them and promise not to let them die (just as well as I have a history of chronic neglect against my own plants, leading to their eventual demise). With the cleaner also on my side, I feel confident to embark on the 'bring the outdoors in' project.

I am reliably informed by my colleague that it is all about picking the right plants. She teaches me (and my pupils) about the difference between foliage and blooming plants and, as a class, we agree that we want both kinds. With a lot of help from Jane we pick out some spider plants, pothos, some coleus for colour and a begonia for its flowers – and for the teaching opportunity of looking at monoecious plants, which have both male and female flowers on the same specimen. It certainly is a learning journey for me!

As we are short of space we pick some foliage plants to live in baskets: the spider and the pothos do very well hanging from our ceiling. In just a few weeks our classroom is looking greener, brighter and more inviting and we have brought some of the benefits of nature right into our room. Now, all I have to do is hope I can keep them alive!

Gardening our way to happiness

After the success of our indoor garden I feel a bit more confident to go back out into the 'wild'. While the forest is still a long way away, this time we are going outdoors with a purpose. There is a small space of earth, currently unused, behind one of the sheds where we keep our sports equipment and, after asking for permission, I propose to the kids that we make it into a garden. It is the beginning of spring, and the primal urge to reconnect with nature is felt by all. With a promise of growth in the air, we take our spades and seeds and head outdoors.

We have missed the ideal planting season for a lot of things, but it is the perfect timing for onions and potatoes and if we wait a bit longer we can also pop in some peas, lettuce and spinach. The children love getting their hands dirty and I am excited by the anticipation of all our veggies. I am even more excited to hear of research at the University of Bristol that found a possible link between a type of bacteria found in soil and the release of the mood-boosting neurotransmitter serotonin. I certainly hope that our garden might become a true mood booster, as well as a learning project, and a haven away from the stresses of the classroom.

 At Home

Start early

Once more, it seems that the Scandinavians have some good ideas on this. My Danish friend has often spoken to me about the habit of leaving babies outside, to sleep in their pram, while the adults are inside having a coffee or shopping. It is a cultural practice that many Scandinavians subscribe to.

Yet, when I take my three week old out in the mild Greek winter, I get stares, then comments about the cold. At first I laugh it off, since it is 7°C, which is hardly freezing. But when I start receiving stern looks and open criticism from other parents, I relent. I still take my little bundle out in our garden, but refrain from doing so in public spaces. As it is peak flu season, indoor spaces are not recommended either, and so . . . home it is. I do, however, take him out for walks around the neighbourhood and, in fact, find that he sleeps better after an afternoon walk. He is also a lot calmer, and cries a lot less when outside: we often end up sitting under the trees in our garden when he refuses to stop crying. It seems that nature, the green rustling leaves and the fresh air are an instant baby calmer.

Make it important – schedule it in

My older son too, seems to love being outdoors. He enjoys playing in the garden, but even a short, daily walk around the neighbourhood is beneficial. I make a point of putting it in the diary: I schedule it in as I do his swimming lesson and our playdates. It is a time of many benefits and I take a similar approach with it, as I (used to) do with my personal fitness regime: whatever the weather we will go out for ten minutes. If after ten minutes we want to come back we can. We rarely return that early, however, as, once the inertia has been overcome, all three of us deeply enjoy being outside.

Some days he rides on the buggy, some days he insists on pushing his brother in it and other times he is adamant he wants to walk. I let him, despite the slow pace, as I see that he actually engages with nature during his walks. He picks flowers, bends down to smell them, collects pine cones and offers them to me as presents. I can see him becoming mindful of the natural world around us.

We try hard to fit in a walk in nature as a family too at least once a week. When we do, my husband and I both notice that our boys change in nature. They become calmer and more attentive. Time in natural surroundings seems to be amplified (in direct contrast to time while engaging in sedentary indoor pursuits, like watching TV, where time seems to just slip away). It also becomes memorable – my toddler seems to remember where we saw that tortoise last time, where he found the tasty berries the time before.

He notices and takes a keen interest in the changes that occur in nature too: the leaves that turn in autumn, the small flowers that are everywhere in early spring. He watches as our olive trees fill with buds, how they turn into flowers, then tiny olives, and he enjoys picking them when the time comes. Joe starts enjoying gardening with his dad, getting his hands dirty and when he gets his own set of gardening tools, a wooden rake and spade which are mini replicas of his dad's, he insists on going out into our small garden every afternoon.

When our kids are a little older, we decide to introduce them to hiking. Before children, walking and running on the mountains near our house was a daily habit that we both relished. It was the perfect way to unwind, forget about the day, disconnect from work and also spend time together. After the arrival of the boys we fell out of the habit but once the boys are old enough we start with short, easy walks. We invest in a baby carrier and head out to the mountains. We are pleasantly surprised at how much the boys enjoy these walks. Joe enjoys picking sticks and leading the way, choosing different paths and scrambling up rocks. He looks forward to the walks, gets to know some of the paths and regular walkers on them and anticipates the short picnic at the end. They become part of our family tradition, something that we do together, reaping the benefits of nature, and the benefit of togetherness and family. However, as winter starts approaching we have another challenge ahead of us.

Get the right equipment

Liisa, my Finnish friend, tells me that there is no bad weather, only bad clothing. She tells me that in Finland children go out to play no matter what the weather and adults join them. In a country where anything above 10°C is considered warm, I find that quite amazing! She laughs when she recalls how long it takes to get in and out of the many layers of clothing in winter, but then adds: 'If it's taken you thirty minutes to get dressed you want to make the most of it!' – and I can see her point.

I decide that the best investment I can make to my commitment for more outdoor time is buying the right equipment. It actually proves fairly easy, with no extremes of temperatures to deal with.

A sun suit and hat for summer, a set of waterproofs and wellies for autumn and winter and some warm gear, mostly scarves, hats and gloves, as well as a warm coat seem to cover most eventualities. I buy most of them second-hand and do not worry much about quality – the kids will only wear them for a short while before growing out of them.

In fact, just this small step really helps change my mindset about the weather and also helps the boys get into the ritual of going outside even more. Joe's wellies become his very favourite shoes, because they get associated with mud, puddles and fun outside. He keeps wearing them well into the next summer, until his feet grow too big to even attempt to put them on. Getting a few items for me too, as well as a buggy cover, means that no weather is prohibitive to us going out and we start enjoying the outdoors almost every day of the year!

Get the right attitude

Appropriately equipped, I start seeing a big attitude change in both me and the boys. My two year old starts asking for 'out' on a daily basis and I find I am happy to go out most of the time. I also start noticing how much part of our routine going out becomes, no matter what the weather, even just for a short half-hour of gardening. The back garden becomes an extension of our house, weather permitting, and we even start going out for some of our meals, on the days that picnics are possible. I also set up a tent in the back and they pretend we are going camping long before we actually dare to take our two little ones on a real camping trip. The back garden, small as it is, becomes an adventure ground for the boys. They dig for worms, and 'cook' with leaves and sticks, they build a shelter in a corner under a tree and I often simply watch them (or read a book) as they enjoy nature, get muddy and explore the world.

 ## Tech it up

Not everyone has easy access to nature but it is easy to bring the outdoors electronically indoors, playing rainforest or wave sounds as background noise or showing scenes of nature on your devices. Why not set up your screensaver or desktop background with a picture of a Norwegian fjord, the Swiss Alps or the English Lake District!

Mindfulness

'Half an hour's meditation each day is essential, except when you are busy. Then a full hour is needed.' *Saint Francis de Sales*

 The Idea

Mindfulness is, at its heart, about learning to better control your attention, and practising doing so in an accepting and kind way. Formal sitting meditations are a way of setting time aside for mindfulness and often use breathing or another bodily sensation as a focus for the attention. Yoga or tai chi add movements, positions and breathing practices to the mindfulness practice.

Both mindfulness and meditation have been hailed as useful tools in the quest for mental and physical well-being and I have been keen to feel their benefits myself. But with all the good intentions in the world I found a regular practice elusive. What was I doing wrong? Does meditation really have a place in our modern, largely secular world? How much time should we be investing in such practices before we start to reap rewards? And, the most difficult question of them all, how on earth am I going to make a group of seven year olds sit still for twenty whole minutes?

The Research

There is lots of evidence that people find mindfulness helpful and that people who undertake a regular mindfulness practice do report feeling happier. But because different people teach and practise mindfulness in different ways, it is hard to know exactly what 'ingredient' in mindfulness is such a boost to happiness.

In the last few years research into mindfulness has exploded, with more than forty new scientific articles and dozens of books being published every month. We are riding the crest of a wave of research into mindfulness – as a therapeutic technique, in popular awareness and, increasingly, in schools. So, what have we learnt from all this research?

In adults, mindfulness-based therapy has been used for many years to improve mental health, particularly in depression, anxiety and eating disorders, and to help people living with chronic pain conditions. In healthy people, learning mindfulness practices seems to help cognitive skills such as concentration, and people report increases in well-being, such as reduced anxiety and finding life more meaningful.

At the moment, no one is really sure how mindfulness produces long-term benefits for well-being. One possibility is that it seems to reduce activity in the default mode network, a circuit in the brain which is active whenever the mind is not concentrating on anything in particular. People with depression tend to show higher levels of activity in this network, and both taking antidepressants and meditating seem to lower its activity. So it may be that by practising maintaining awareness of the present moment, you change the brain's 'idle' mechanism, over time reducing the activity in this background mind-wandering network.

As the success of mindfulness became obvious, programmes have been adapted or developed for use specifically with young people. In the last few years there have been some very well-designed trials looking at the effects of simple mindfulness programmes in children as young as preschoolers, and the use of other mindfulness-related practices such as tai chi and yoga in older children and teenagers. Taken as a whole, the evidence suggests that teaching mindfulness in schools helps students' cognitive performance, stress and resilience – great news for teachers, parents and kids alike.

Regardless of how much good it does in the long term, one reason that mindfulness seems to have become so popular is that it tends to help you feel better right from the start. This is important because we know that humans are not great at denying instant pleasure for longer-term rewards. Lots of the things we know we should do (choose salad instead of chips, go to the gym instead of watching TV) have long-term benefits but aren't so attractive in the short term. With mindfulness, it probably is the case that people who practise more will see bigger changes. But the great news is that even a short practice – one that fits into a busy day – can give you a quick boost of calm, relaxation and happiness.

PRACTISING THE HAPPINESS HABIT

 ### *At School*

Sssshhh! It is completely quiet. It's late afternoon and I am sitting on the carpet in my classroom, surrounded by twenty seven year olds all absolutely absorbed in their mindfulness practice. For the last twenty minutes they have all been sitting completely still and quiet, eyes shut. Nobody's stirring, nobody is moving. We are meditating.

Only this is not the real world. If you have even the slightest experience of children you probably know that a twenty-minute silent practice is out of the question. It becomes quite clear to me early in my attempt to introduce some mindfulness into my daily classroom schedule: traditional sit-down contemplative practice does not work for (my) kids – if anything it frustrates both me and them.

I am, however, already seeing the benefits of a regular, short practice of sitting meditation in my own life. I am calmer, happier to accept things as they are and less likely to get wound up by things that do not matter. I want my pupils to have a glimpse into this; if nothing else it would make for a much calmer and friendlier teaching environment.

My early attempts all fail miserably. It is clear that I am not an expert in mindfulness and am lacking in the depth of knowledge to apply this beneficial practice in our everyday school life. I have my work cut out: I will have to do my research and find some child-friendly ways to bring mindfulness into our busy days. With that in mind, I go to chat to an expert.

Maria has been teaching meditation to children and teenagers for more than ten years. She has her own yoga studio, where I join her for a class with my toddler (more on that later) but she also goes to schools, youth camps and even teaches at a local kinder-garten. She explains to me something that I have noticed already, but she puts it into words for me: children are already open to mindfulness meditation because they spend more of their time in a state she calls 'open awareness'. I agree with that and share with her the sort of activities I envisage we could do in class. She endorses some of them, and suggests I scale back some of my other efforts. At the end of the day we don't want kids to be struggling or feel that they are failing at mindfulness. A clear focus of attention and open awareness is all we are aiming for. In terms of time she suggests that a good amount is one minute per year of the child's age. That all sounds doable. Before I leave she reminds me of my commitment to come and join one of her classes with my son, and I agree.

Mindfulness using the senses

Mindfulness is a good starting point for trying meditative practices, as it is easier to introduce to children. The moment I start being more mindful and sharing it with the kids, though, I notice something: my pupils (and it later transpired, kids in general) tend to be a lot more mindful than adults. It is probably because, for children, a lot of the world is brand new – they are often naturally a lot more aware, a lot more awake to their experiences. I notice it one day when, as we walk into our classroom, several children remark on the 'yummy cookie smell'. That comment makes me search out the smell, which turns out to be vanilla perfume on my scarf, left over from another day.

Once I have noticed that children have an inclination towards mindfulness, all I need is to make them aware of their . . . awareness. I talk to them about being present in the moment, again something I feel that they know more about than me. They agree to play a game with me: every time I ring a little bell I have by my desk they have to focus on all the sounds they can hear, outside of themselves for a minute. I then ring the bell again to bring them back. We rotate our senses, trying to take everything in. One week it is sound, the next it is smell and the week after that we concentrate on what we can see. This happens once or twice a day.

When it comes to the week of taste, I decide to do a more practical exercise that is suggested in Mark Williams and Danny Penman's excellent book *Mindfulness: A Practical Guide to Finding Peace in a Frantic World* and which I have practised at home several times. It involves chocolate, so it is one that I keep on coming back to and one that I think the kids will enjoy!

After making sure that no one in my class has a nut allergy and that they are allowed to eat it, I bring in two bars of chocolate. I sit with the kids, after their lunch, and slowly cut the chocolate into enough pieces so everyone can have one. I share with them the point of the exercise: although we often have a treat, today's treat we are really going to savour. We will look at it, smell it and then slowly put it in our mouths, where we will let it melt, while really tasting it. A special, mindful kind of treat.

I want the kids to approach the exercise with curiosity and playfulness. I don't expect any feedback or comments, this is just for them to experience and simply be present in the moment. It has worked for me every time I have tried it and I am keen to share it with the kids.

This first time, I lead the children through the exercise by reading out loud to them a little script with the steps on it. The next time I try it, I write the instructions on the board and do the exercise in silence. The time after that I let the kids guide their own experience.

After everyone has swallowed their piece we have a very brief discussion about the experience. How did it make everyone feel? Was it different to the way they usually eat? To my last question: 'Would you like to repeat the experience?' I get a resounding yes!

Trying to inject some mindfulness into our days, as well as gratitude for all we have, can be combined easily during our communal lunch break. Spending a minute each day tasting our food, *really* tasting it, at the beginning of each meal, is an easy thing to do. And so our daily eating mindfulness becomes a reality – the first minute of each lunchtime is spent looking at, smelling and then tasting our first mouthful. It might not be quite as pleasurable as the chocolate, but it is an easy way to bring the moment into focus and increase our mindfulness.

On top of the mindful moment at the beginning of each meal I try to keep the weekly theme of senses, and to encourage children to share some of their mindful moments. In that way the roughness of the carpet on bare legs, felt tens of times every day, is brought into sharp focus on the 'feeling/touching' week. The smell of jasmine that permeates our playground at certain times of year, is noticed and shared on the 'smelling' week. And we all become a lot more aware of the brightness of the sky, or the funny shapes of clouds on the 'seeing' weeks.

Back to basics

Being more mindful is going well, but setting aside time for a dedicated meditation practice poses more of a challenge. After a lot of thinking and reading I decide to start with the very basics: the breath. The breath is often at the centre of many meditation exercises. But meditation has to somehow become fun for these kids, not simply one more thing they need to do. So I recruit Freddy. Freddy is my resident (toy) frog – a gift from a dear friend. He has been my teaching companion for the last seven years, and kids adore him, as he injects fun into maths and English (you see, he really struggled with his adverbs and adjectives and kids love to teach him stuff). It is time for Freddy to start meditation classes. But he can't do it alone: I ask the kids to each bring into school one small stuffed toy who will become their meditation friend.

Teddies, doggies and other toy animals in tow, we all lie down on the carpet. Our meditation friends are placed on our bellies and we observe them as they rise and fall, rise and fall. With each breath the teddies move up, then fall down as we exhale. All I want is for a few minutes of silence, while we watch our furry friends dancing to the rhythm of our breathing. I remember Maria's advice about the duration of our meditation sessions: one minute for each year of age, but even after several practice sessions I decide that four minutes is enough – not so long that children get restless yet long enough for them to immerse themselves in the breath and silence of meditation.

Another practice that I think might work with the kids is a variation on the flame meditation technique. This involves using a lit candle to help focus the mind, letting go of thoughts and simply watching the flickering of the flame. The act of concentrating on something physical can make this kind of meditation more accessible so it is a good one for beginners. My insurmountable challenge is that open flames are a no-no in the classroom. Even if they were allowed, I am not foolish enough to introduce ten lit candles to twenty active children. I am having a hard time coming up with an alternative, though, so for the time being I shelve the idea.

It is coming up to Christmas, and I am spending a rushed couple of hours trying to decorate my tree. Joe is helping me, pulling decorations out of their boxes and carefully inspecting them before handing some of them to me to hang up on our tree. Oliver is also 'helping' by chewing on a plastic reindeer. Anyone with a toddler knows that more than two minutes of silence can be a sign of trouble, and so I am slightly worried when I realise that the living room has been silent for several minutes already. I look for Joe, hoping that he is not eating the Christmas lights, or feeding the baby tinsel, only to find him lying on his tummy, his head propped up on his hands, intently watching something. That something is a snow globe, its flakes softly twirling around with a life of their own. I watch him observe them, lost in their dance and then, once they settle, pick up the snow globe and shake it again, starting the process once more.

It hits me: this is it! The flame meditation has just found a reincarnation in the snow globe meditation. A little less risky, but just as engrossing, the snow globes become our favourite meditation tool. The children even make their own snow globes with jars, glycerine and glitter, and variations thereof.

It is important to me that meditation does not simply become another task, and certainly not something that you can either do or not do. From my own practice I have seen just how critical I can become of myself, and how I often have thoughts of failure if I cannot empty my mind, or if thoughts keep popping into my head. Meditation is not meant to be like that. I find it useful to use the analogy of my mind as a sky, and my thoughts as clouds travelling in it – this image reminds me that it is very natural to have thoughts on my mind – that my mind is their natural space, but that I can simply observe them, rather than engage with them. I am keen to help children understand that every minute spent in this kind of state is useful, the point of the exercise is simply to observe and there is no right or wrong.

Like clouds in the sky

For that reason I make a meditation worksheet . . . I know, it sounds like I am missing the point a bit, but bear with me. The sheet depicts a sky, and there are clouds on it. I ask the children to draw or write one word, representing their thoughts, inside one of the clouds. Then, without thinking any further, move onto the next one, and then the one after that. They do this for three minutes. In this way they can be observing, in a non-judgemental way, the weather pattern of their minds. I enjoy this one a lot and often join in. When the three minutes are up we take our sheet, fold it, crumple it or simply leave it as it is, and throw it away.

My final exercise is probably my favourite, in that if I had to choose just one type of meditation for school this would be it. Compassion meditation is a mainstay of the Buddhist tradition and is used to open up the mind and heart to being more compassionate to others and ourselves. In its simplest form, it involves focusing your attention on one person, helping cultivate feelings of warmth and gratitude towards them.

I am pleased to see that the children enjoy both our moments of mindfulness and our brief meditation sessions. They all find

154

something in them, even if they struggle to maintain engagement. If I am honest, I can't say that mindfulness or meditation makes my classroom quieter or calmer. I know that our mindfulness sessions definitely bring a playfulness and curiosity into our everyday encounters, as well as a higher degree of sharing experiences. I am happy that, according to the research, practising meditation can be a stress-reliever and I hope I am offering the children another tool to deal with the ups and downs of life. This one is going to be a gift that keeps on giving, aside from whatever benefits it has on our classroom vibe.

 ## At Home

The yoga class

I want to take these experiences into my home but I feel like, for this one, I need some help from the experts. I join Maria in her yoga studio for a class of toddler and adult yoga. The class is well attended, and we are the only newcomers here today. I take a spot right at the back and, instead of feeling calm and collected I find myself agitated. I realise that my rising anxiety is to do with my expectations of Joe's behaviour and, as I see the rest of the children grab their mats I wonder if this session will end up being more tantrum yoga than toddler yoga.

Maria starts with a speech aimed at exactly me: I wonder if she has been able to read my mind. She talks about managing expectations, about the fact that 'hey, they are only two or three years old!' and that if we get two or three poses that would be a success. I feel myself visibly relax. My tense shoulders drop and I let out a long exhalation. Even as she is talking one of the youngest participants has lain down and seems to be asleep, while another is trying to climb on the stack of mats at the end of the room. It will be fine.

Joe is happy in my arms, where he often stays when he is unsure of his surroundings. When we sit in a circle, our legs open and (most of) our kids sitting between our legs, he is happy to sit close to mummy. Thirty-five minutes later, after a lesson I would not have recognised as yoga, I get a chance to chat to Maria again, while Joe spends a good ten minutes watching the fish in her fish tank swim serenely around.

While Maria tells me about the benefits of the practice, I have to say I remain unconvinced. She tells me about the stretching and the mindfulness, but I don't think Joe did much of either of those. She highlights the chance to do something physical together and, although I do think that is a worthwhile goal, I leave the yoga lesson fairly convinced that this is not the activity for Joe and me. We will have to find some other way to bring meditation into our family life.

Mindfulness in nature

We spend a lot of time outside in nature. It is where I find my calm and where my husband and I have, for years, enjoyed spending a lot of our free time. Now that the kids are here we find no reason to change what we see as such a positive habit. We are lucky enough to have a garden and most days, weather permitting, we spend time out there. For purely selfish reasons, I find it a lot easier to look after the children outside: they tend to find their own activities and get engrossed in them easily, their free play tends to be more imaginative and they are usually calmer and happier when we are outside. I think this is a good setting to look for ways to introduce mindfulness and meditation to them.

I don't expect Joe to sit down and focus for any amount of time, but simply for us both to be more aware of our surroundings. If anything he seems more mindful of the nature around us than I am. Once in a while, during our outdoor play sessions, I ask him to sit with me and I talk to him about the sounds that surround us. Then we play a simple listening game. The great thing about focusing on the sounds around us is that sound can only happen in the present: it is the perfect way to bring us into the moment. I remember Maria's instructions of one minute of meditation per age of the child and we sit there for a couple of minutes, soaking up all the sounds around us. Joe loves to share any sound that enters into his awareness: the dog that barks, the rustling of the leaves in the wind, the buzzing of the bee. Then he notices the aeroplane, and the car that is driving off in the distance. He hears the sound of the water pump, as my husband turns on a tap inside the house, and then back to the buzzing of the bee and the rustling of the leaves. It's a grounding activity and I find myself greatly enjoying our very own garden meditation. The more we do it the more Joe finds it easier to get into, easier to approach with open awareness and soak in the sounds. Maria's recommended two minutes often become five and there is even the odd occasion when we just lose sense of time and get drawn into our sense of hearing in the here and now.

After several goes at listening in nature, I get another idea, as Joe points out a passing aeroplane to me. We lie down on the grass and spend a few minutes looking at the passing clouds: he is fascinated by them and I love lying here next to him, watching as the white puffs travel and drift past us. I find the experience deeply satisfying and I spend the rest of the morning feeling very grounded. Maybe some cloud gazing has done us both good!

My kind of mindfulness: colouring in

I am at Krista's house for coffee. She is a busy mother of three feisty kids and it is nice to be in her company. She seems to be one of those do-it-all mums, but I am pleased to see that her house is no tidier than mine and her kids also have cereal for dinner from time to time. Phew! We have been chatting about breakfast bar recipes, or rather she has been telling me about hers and I am hesitant to join in the conversation because I know it is highly unlikely that I will ever sit down and bake my own granola bars. Still, while she is looking for a piece of paper to copy the recipe down for me we come across sheets and sheets of intricately coloured-in pages. I just have to ask what they are and her answer astounds me.

'This is me practising mindfulness,' she informs me and I wonder if I heard her right. She shows me page after page of printed designs, some of nature, some of simple repeating patterns, all painstakingly coloured in.

'This one is Lucy's,' she shows me another piece, coloured in beautifully in pastels. Her eleven year old has obviously spent quite a long time working on it. I want to know more.

'Well, I started using colouring-in mindfulness for myself,' she explains, 'but soon enough the kids wanted to join in. So I print out a few pages each week and every two to three days we sit down, at the kitchen table, and we just colour in. Most of the time in silence, sometimes we put some music on.'

Colouring-in mindfulness for the whole family! Krista assures me that it is a sure-fire stress buster and, just before I leave, she gives me a couple of sheets, as well as the granola bar recipe. I am not sure if I will manage to use the latter, but the colouring-in meditation has captured my imagination. I used to love colouring in as a child and only recently I caught myself envying my eldest as he concentrated ever so hard to stay within the lines of an aquatic themed colouring page, so I vow to give them a go.

A couple of days later, while Joe is deeply engrossed in picking the right colours, I bring out my very own colouring page. He glances over at me, and without much thought hands me one of his pencils. Soon we are both colouring, in complete silence in our kitchen. When my husband comes in and asks what we are doing I explain to him that we are meditating and he gives me a questioning look. I need to get him involved too!

As I get in touch with my inner child, I start to really enjoy my colouring, but most of all I start enjoying sharing this quiet time with Joe. I sometimes watch him as he colours and I can see that he is totally lost in the moment.

I start thinking about the pointlessness of the exercise, I catch myself thinking what a waste of time it is and then it dawns on me: that is *exactly* the point! We very rarely do anything for the sake of it – most of our actions every day are goal driven. This kind of active meditation is meant to focus attention on this simple but repetitive task and promote inner peace and relaxation. I know it works for me, and looking across at Joe too, I can see it is working for him. This certainly is my kind of meditation!

 ## Tech it up

You and your teenagers might enjoy using a soundtrack to help you meditate, and there are also several apps available to get you into the habit, providing guided meditations for different situations and lengths of time. Some apps also provide periods of timed silence, removing the need to worry about keeping track of time.

Recycling Happiness

"'Oh, Marilla, looking forward to things is half
the pleasure of them," exclaimed Anne. "You
mayn't get the things themselves; but nothing
can prevent you from having the fun of looking
forward to them.'"   *Lucy Maud Montgomery*

 The Idea

Sharing news, reflecting on life and anticipating events can
enhance children's happiness.

As every primary school teacher knows (and every parent should
be warned about, before their kids start school), children love to
share their news. From the mundane fact that the new hamster
eats its own poo, to the rather more interesting one that daddy
was wearing mummy's underwear last night (true story), teachers
hear it all. Such conversations come easily to children, both in
class and in the playground and hardly need to be encouraged.

Ask a five year old to share his news and you will usually get a cascade of their latest adventures.

When I first started teaching one of the things I noticed about children was how they often used past and future events to intuitively maximise their own happiness. I learnt a lot about the nature of happiness from watching children get excited about simple things like their birthday party, days and sometimes weeks or months in advance. In fact, one of the things that really stayed with me was how the mere anticipation of that event seemed to affect children's happiness levels. The effect seemed to be naturally magnified when we shared such news and it seemed that our collective happiness level would be raised by spreading the excitement of the anticipated event.

We are often told that 'sharing is caring' and that 'if you laugh, the world will laugh with you', but can simply sharing our good news enhance our levels of well-being? Can looking forward to an event and talking about it, make us that little bit happier? And if so, what's the best way to share? How often should we do it and with whom? And finally, how can we fit that into our busy everyday lives?

The Research

An event can affect us three times over: in anticipating it, living through it and then recollecting it. It makes sense then that a lot of the sum total of happiness experienced in life comes from the pleasure of expectation, and of remembering. (Of course this is equally true for unpleasant sensations: one reason why many people find mindfulness helpful is that by concentrating on the here-and-now, we can reduce the time spent worrying about the future or dwelling on what has already passed.)

There can be a real contrast between our feelings about past and future experiences and the emotions that we actually experience at the time. A child may dread an upcoming exam or not want to go to a party, but then enjoy it when it actually comes to pass. This potential for misaligned emotions is really important. Whether we think about an upcoming event as fearful or exciting can have a big influence on how that event will be experienced. And while we obviously cannot change the past, our feelings about past events often change considerably over time as we relive them with others, or as new information comes to light.

The boost to happiness that can be gained from anticipating a future event is surprisingly powerful, in some cases larger than the happiness gained from the event itself. One study of a thousand Dutch people looked at the effect that going on holiday has on happiness. It found that people who were about to go on holiday were – unsurprisingly – happier than those who did not have this event to look forward to. When questioned again on their return, however, people who had just been on holiday were in fact no happier than those who had not. In another large study, this one in Britain, people were surveyed about their happiness and satisfaction before and after major life events such as getting married. As you would expect, newly-weds of both sexes reported an immediate boost in happiness. There were striking differences between the sexes, however. Women but not men showed a large anticipatory effect: on average their happiness was at a higher level for more than one year leading up the wedding day and it didn't return to its original level for more than four years after the wedding. Engaged men, however, showed little anticipatory happiness in the build-up to a wedding, and adapted back to their usual levels of happiness within a year of marriage.

So for some events in life, anticipation can clearly be a major source of happiness. What effect does retelling an experience have on happiness after the event? Well it probably depends a lot on the way we recount the event. We know that the way we tell stories about our lives can colour our feelings about those past events. When talking to children about things that have happened, we have a big opportunity to affect how they understand past events: careful studies analysing conversations between parents and children show that the way that parents tell stories has a big influence on the way children then talk about those events.

Laboratory studies have also shown another very important thing about recycling good news – that it's worth picking the right person to tell it to. As you might expect, the happiness associated with good news is increased by sharing it with it someone, preferably someone you are close to. But how that person responds is really important: receiving an enthusiastic response gives an additional boost to happiness. Worth bearing in mind when an excited child is competing with other calls on your attention!

PRACTISING THE HAPPINESS HABIT

 ## *At School*

Every class teacher has a morning routine and it usually, inevitably, includes the taking of a register. A lot of teachers do this in a perfunctory manner – after all, there is usually a backlog of targets and actual teaching to get on with. For me it has always been a chance to say good morning to each child individually and connect on a human level, before the busy day gets underway.

The register ritual

I would like to see it as less of a routine and more of a ritual. It goes something like this: as I say good morning to each pupil, I ask them to give me a rating, from one to ten, on how happy they are that day. It soon becomes the class's favourite activity and is in fact a great incentive for children to come to school on time – many a time parents have commented on their child's insistence on getting into school before the bell went, signalling the end of the registration ritual.

The reason that I insist on this ritual is twofold: first, I feel that sharing such news strengthens our connections as a group, making each and every one of us feel a part of this special community: our class. Second, I want the children to recycle their happiness, to get as much happiness out of each event as they possibly can. Anticipation can be a strong driver of happiness for us all. From early October on, children mention countless times that they are excited that Christmas is coming. While this seems to go against the idea of living in the moment, I often share their excitement and it is contagious!

Looking forward

Another way that we recycle happiness is by regularly writing about what we are looking forward to. I am amazed to see how, with practice, children get better at this and start looking forward to even the smallest things in life. Sometimes it is an ice cream after school, sometimes the visit of a grandparent, sometimes simple anticipation of the weekend, or breaktime, or a particularly yummy snack for the day. The mere thought of it elevates our collective mood, making children happier in that moment.

Looking back

Reflection on events works differently and again this forms part of our morning routine, where children can mention events that have made them happy. It could be a funny story that happened to them on their way to school, or something their little brother said. Sharing such nuggets brings us all closer together, helps us share a laugh and engages us all in a positive mindset.

Of course life is not all sunshine and unicorns. Occasionally we have sad news, from the more benign (I lost my favourite pencil) to the life-changing (my grandpa died). It is important to share that tough news too; important to speak about it and exorcise it in some way. Unhappy stories are peppered amongst other stories, and we, as a community, still share them, so that children know they have someone to share their bad news with, as well as their good. It is important that, from a young age, we learn that just as life can be full of happiness, it can also be tough.

Again, this process brings us all closer together and acts as a support to all of us. The good and bad tends to balance out and at the end of the day everyone knows that no matter what happens, there is always someone to chat to about the good, the bad and the ugly.

At Home

It is Father's Day today. We have a rule that we do not buy presents for such occasions: we either make something or do something together. But Joe is very excited! We are preparing a special breakfast for Daddy, complete with heart-shaped waffles and honey, Daddy's favourite coffee and vanilla milk for the boys and, not to forget, colourful bunting decorating our kitchen.

Before we had kids Duncan and I seldom celebrated any occasion. Looking back over several years of being together I can hardly remember any of our anniversaries, birthdays or even Christmases. When Joe joined us it became one of my resolutions to start celebrating more, making some special memories for him and us.

Make special days

Some of the occasions we celebrate are official events, like Father's Day. But we also celebrate 'First Ice cream of the Summer Day' and 'Going to the Beach Fridays'. We have 'Godmother's Sunday' and the ever-welcome 'Start of the Weekend Pizza Night' which happens every Friday.

These special days help us mark time in a fun way, but we get a lot more happiness out of them by anticipating them too. I am always happy to remember that today is pizza Friday, or that in five days' time it will be 'First Ice cream of the Summer Day'. Which brings me nicely to the second point:

Buy a calendar and count down

It is clear that part of the pleasure we derive from special occasions like holidays is from the anticipation and build-up towards the event. And so I decide that I will have a special calendar, hanging up in our kitchen, showing all these wonderful occasions.

Next to our regular calendar I hang another one. This one is certainly more fun and it has big squares for each day, waiting to be filled. It will not have our dentist's appointments, or Oliver's next inoculation date. Instead we spend some time each week putting in all the happy occasions: birthdays, party days, last days of school, first days of school, holidays like Christmas and Easter, planned trips and visits and some made up days too.

I remember from my childhood the sheer excitement of looking forward to things: birthdays, Christmas, a holiday. I remember counting sleeps and, as the date approached, the sheer delight I took in going to bed at night and getting closer to the longed-for date. I loved this intense anticipation and I want my boys to share in it with me, so we start using our calendar to look forward to upcoming events. I make sure that the boys get involved in the preparations too: before a holiday we start packing our bags with seven sleeps to go, before a friend's birthday party we go together to choose a present, before Daddy's birthday they help me make cakes. They love being involved and I can see how it amplifies the happiness from the experience alone and help it permeate the rest of our life!

Remember and re-create happy memories

My final intervention is one that I found the most challenging. Before mobile phones contained cameras I never owned a camera, digital or otherwise. I am one of these people who strongly believe that life is for enjoying and not for taking pictures of. Whether it was out of laziness or truly a way of looking at life, I don't know, but I have very few pictures of the years between when my parents stopped taking pictures of us as kids, around the age of fifteen, and my thirties when I got a camera phone. Even once I had a camera phone, I rarely got pictures printed, leaving any memories that I captured trapped in electronic form for ever.

For the boys' first Christmas I decide to change that. After some thought, I resolve to make several copies of an album for each year that passed, and give them to family as presents. I will not lie: it takes quite a bit of work! (I have since found internet sites where you send your pictures electronically and they bind them for you in a book – fantastic!) But it is very much worth it and the grand-mothers especially love a printed reminder of all the happy times together. I also keep a copy for us, and enjoy looking at it regularly with the boys. In fact, maybe I will make up a 'Happy Memories Day' where we spend time looking over all our pictures!

 Tech it up

Most electronic devices and email accounts have electronic calendars. Many can be shared with members of a family so that everyone can see upcoming events. You can even set up regular notifications to go out to members of your group, to make sure that nobody forgets, but also to help everyone share in the happy feelings that anticipation can bring. As for re-creating happy memories: getting one of those e-frames that plays a slideshow of all pictures means that you can have some of your favourite photos showing all the time, but easily change them as you create more and more memories with your loved ones!

Afterthought

We all know (but sometimes forget) that in parenting, as with life in general, there are no guarantees, no foolproof solutions. A lot of what we do as parents is simply try different things and see if they work. Sometimes they do, sometimes they don't. On top of that, what works now might not work a few months down the line, and what works for one of our kids might not work for another. Parenting is an exploration, an adventure, sometimes tough and oftentimes exasperating but in the end, for most of us, the wildest ride ever!

The guidance that we receive as parents is invaluable but should come without judgement, be it from a book, a professional or from a friend who is further down the road in the parenting game. We hope this book has done just that, given you a few more things to try, things that will hopefully translate positively to your children, grandchildren, nephews, nieces – or any children you care deeply about. We also hope that you have enjoyed playing around with the ideas suggested in the book, and have even discovered a few of your own ways to put happiness habits into your daily lives in ways that fit around your family and your rituals.

A perfect childhood is unattainable. But even If it were possible, I often try to remind myself that it would probably not be my choice for my kids: children develop resilience and learn valuable lessons in those first years of life, including from things that go wrong. We all make mistakes when parenting and we all need to be reassured that those mistakes very rarely translate to bad outcomes for our kids. Children need to grow up in a loving, caring home where their needs are consistently met. The rest is icing on the cake. Having fun with that icing is what this book is about!

As many mums do, in preparation for having kids, but also for writing this book, Jenny and I read a lot of books that focus on particular aspects of parenting, happiness or both. Here is a list with some of them that we found particularly helpful, and hope you might enjoy too. May your days be filled with joy!

Burkeman, Oliver, *Help: How to Become Slightly Happier and Get a Bit More Done* (Canongate Books, 2011).

Cohen, Lawrence J., *Playful Parenting* (Ballantine Books, 2012).

Csikszentmihalyi, Mihaly, *Flow: The Psychology of Happiness* (Rider, 2002).

DeBenedet, Anthony and Lawrence J. Cohen, *The Art of Roughhousing: Good Old-Fashioned Horseplay and Why Every Kid Needs It* (Quirk Books, 2010).

Gilbert, Dan, *Stumbling on Happiness* (Harper Perennial, 2007).

Haidt, Richard, *The Happiness Hypothesis: Putting Ancient Wisdom to the Test of Modern Science* (Arrow, 2007)

Layard, Richard, *Happiness: Lessons from a New Science* (Penguin, 2011).

Louv, Richard, *Last Child in the Woods* (Atlantic Books, 2013).

Milligan, Spike, *Silly Verse for Kids* (Puffin, 1973).

Rubin, Gretchen, *Happier at Home: Kiss More, Jump More, Abandon a Project, Read Samuel Johnson, and My Other Experiments in the Practice of Everyday Life* (Two Roads, 2013).

Schwartz, Barry, *The Paradox of Choice: Why More is Less* (Harper Perennial, 2007).

Seligman, Martin, *Authentic Happiness: Using the New Positive Psychology to Realise your Potential for Lasting Fulfilment* (Nicholas Brealy Publishing, 2011).

BIBLIOGRAPHY BY CHAPTER

INTRODUCTION

Ashby F., A. Isen and A. Turken , 'A neuropsychological theory of positive affect and its influence on cognition', *Psychological Review* (529–550, 1999).

Boehm, J. and S. Lyubomirsky, 'Does Happiness Promote Career Success?', *Journal of Career Assessment* (101–116, 2008).

Brown, R., 'Children's Eating Attitudes and Behaviour: A Study of the Modelling and Control Theories of Parental Influence', *Health Education Research* (261–271, 2003).

Buchanan, K. and A. Bardi, 'Acts of Kindness and Acts of Novelty Affect Life Satisfaction', *The Journal of Social Psychology* (235–237, 2010).

Esseily, R., L. Rat-Fischer, E. Somogyi, K. O'Regan and J. Fagard, 'Humour production may enhance observational learning of a new tool-use action in 18-month-old infants', *Cognition and Emotion* (1–9, 2015).

Fleeson, W., A. Malanos and N. Achille, 'An intraindividual process approach to the relationship between extraversion and positive affect: Is acting extraverted as "good" as being extraverted?', *Journal of Personality and Social Psychology* (1409–1422, 2002).

Okada, M., M. Kawamura, Y. Kaihara, Y. Matsuzaki, S. Kuwahara, H. Ishidori, H. and K. Miura, 'Influence of Parents' Oral Health Behaviour on Oral Health Status of their School Children: An Exploratory Study Employing a Causal Modelling Technique', *International Journal of Paediatric Dentistry* (101–108, 2002).

SMILES

Ekman, P., *Telling Lies: Clues to Deceit in the Marketplace, Politics, and Marriage* (WW Norton, 1985).

Grossmann, T., 'The development of emotion perception in face and voice during infancy', *Restorative Neurology and Neuroscience* (28, 219–236, 2010).

Gunnery, S. D. and M. A. Ruben, 'Perceptions of Duchenne and non-Duchenne smiles: A meta-analysis', *Cognition and Emotion* (19 March 2015, electronic publication ahead of print).

Mukamel, R., A. D. Ekstrom, J. Kaplan, M. Iacoboni and I. Fried, 'Single-neuron responses in humans during execution and observation of actions', *Current Biology* (20, 750–775, 2010).

Niedenthal, P. M., 'Embodying emotion', *Science* (316, 1002–1005, 2007).

Parr, L. A., B. M. Waller and J. Fugate, 'Emotional communication in primates: implications for neurobiology', *Current Opinion in Neurobiology* (6, 716–720, 2005).

Proverbio, A. M., F. Riva, L. Paganelli, S. F. Cappa, N. Canessa, D. Perani and A. Zani, 'Neural coding of cooperative vs. affective human interactions: 150 ms to code the action's purpose', *PLoS One* (7, e22026, 2011).

Strack, F., L. L. Martin and S. Stepper, 'Inhibiting and facilitating conditions of the human smile: a nonobtrusive test of the facial feedback hypothesis', *Journal of Personality and Social Psychology* (54, 768, 1988).

GRATITUDE

Algoe, S. B., J. Haidt and S. L. Gable, 'Beyond reciprocity: Gratitude and relationships in everyday life', *Emotion* (8, 425–429, 2008).

Emmons, R. A. and M. E. McCullough, 'Counting blessings versus burdens: An experimental investigation of gratitude and subjective well-being in daily life', *Journal of Personality and Social Psychology* (84, 377–389, 2003).

Froh, J. J., W. J. Sefick and R. A. Emmons, 'Counting blessings in early adolescents: An experimental study of gratitude and subjective well-being', *Journal of School Psychology* (46, 213–233, 2008).

Froh, J. J., T. B. Kashdan, K. M. Ozimkowski and N. Miller, 'Who benefits the most from a gratitude intervention in children and adolescents? Examining positive affect as a moderator', *Journal of Positive Psychology* (4, 408–422, 2009).

Wood, A. M. , J. J. Froh and A. W. A. Geraghty, 'Gratitude and well-being: A review and theoretical integration', *Clinical Psychology Review* (30, 7, 890–905, 2010).

SINGING

Bonilha, A. G., F. Onofre, L. M. Vieira, M. Y. A. Almeida Prado and J. A. B. Martinez, 'Effects of singing classes on pulmonary function and quality of life of COPD patients', *International Journal of COPD* (4, 1–8, 2008).

Bungay, H. and T. Vella-Burrows, 'The effects of participating in creative activities on the health and well-being of children and young people: a rapid review of the literature', *Perspectives in Public Health* (133, 1, 44–52, 2013).

Catterall, J. E., R. Chapleau and G. Iwanaga 'Involvement in the Arts and Human Development: General Involvement in Music, Theatre,

Arts', Imagination Project UCLA, School of Education and Information Studies (1999).

Clift, S. and G. Hancox, 'The significance of choral singing for sustaining psychological well-being: Findings from a survey of choristers in England, Australia and Germany', *Music Performance Research* (3, 79–96, 2010).

Cohen, G. D., S. Perlstein, J. Chapline, J. Kelly, K. M. Firth and S. Simmens, 'The impact of professionally conducted cultural programs on the physical health, mental health and social functioning of older adults', *Gerontologist* (46, 726–734, 2006).

Dunbar R. I., K. Kaskatis, I. MacDonald and V. Barra, 'Performance of music elevates pain threshold and positive affect: implications for the evolutionary function of music', *Evolutionary Psychology* (10, 4, 688–702, 2012).

Elefant, C., F. A. Baker, M. Lotan, S. K. Lagesen and G. O. Skeie, 'The effect of group music therapy on mood, speech, and singing in individuals with Parkinson's disease – a feasibility study', *Journal of Music Therapy* (49, 3, 278–302, 2012).

Grape, C., M. Sandgren, L. O. Hansson, M. Ericson and T. Theorell, 'Does singing promote well-being?: An empirical study of professional and amateur singers during a singing lesson', *Integrative Physiological and Behavioral Science* (38, 1, 65–74, 2003).

Kreutz, G., S. Bongard, S. Rohrmann, V. Hodapp and D. Grebe, 'Effects of choir singing or listening on secretory immunoglobulin

A, cortisol, and emotional state', *Journal of Behavioural Medicine* (27, 6, 623–635, 2004).

Lord, V. M., P. Cave, V. Hume, E. J. Flude, A. Evans and J. L. Kelly, 'Singing teaching as a therapy for chronic respiratory disease: Randomised controlled trial and qualitative evaluation', *BMC Pulmonary Medicine* (10, 41, 2010).

McDermott, O., N. Crellin, H. M. Ridder and M. Orrell, 'Music therapy in dementia: a narrative synthesis systematic review', *International Journal of Geriatric Psychiatry* (28, 8, 781–794, 2013).

Skingley, A. and H. Bungay, 'The Silver Song Club Project: Singing to promote the health of older people', *British Journal of Community Nursing* (15, 135–140, 2010).

Tamplin, J., F. A. Baker, D. Grocke, D. J. Brazzale, J. J. Pretto, W. R. Ruehland, M. Buttifant, D. J. Brown and D. J. Berlowitz, 'Effect of singing on respiratory function, voice, and mood after quadri-plegia: a randomized controlled trial', *Archives of Physical Medicine and Rehabilitation* (94, 3, 426–434, 2013).

FINDING MEANING

Aknin, K. B., J. K. Hamlin and E. W. Dunn, 'Giving leads to happiness in young children', *PLoS One* (7, 6, e39211, 2012).

Aknin, L. B., E. W. Dunn, G. M. Sandstrom and M. I. Norton, 'Does social connection turn good deeds into good feelings? On the value of putting the "social" in prosocial spending', *International Journal of Happiness and Development* (1, 2, 155–171, 2013).

Dunn, J., 'Connections between relationships: Implications of research on mothers and siblings', in R. A. Hinde and J. Stevenson-Hinde (eds.), *Relationships within Families: Mutual influences* (168–180, Oxford University Press, 1988).

Hamlin, J. K., K. Wynn and P. Bloom, 'Social evaluation by preverbal infants', *Nature* (450, 557–559, 2007).

Lu, J., C. Huet and L. Dubé, 'Emotional reinforcement as a protective factor for healthy eating in home settings', *American Journal of Clinical Nutrition* (94, 1, 254–261, 2011).

Lyubomirsky, S., K. M. Sheldon and D. Schkade, 'Pursuing happiness: The architecture of sustainable change', *Review of General Psychology* (9, 2, 111–131, 2005).

McConnell, A., C. Brown, T. Shoda, C. Martin and L. Stayton, 'Friends with benefits: On the positive consequences of pet ownership', *Journal of Personality and Social Psychology* (101, 6, 1239–1252, 2011).

Olson, K. R. and E. S. Spelke, 'Foundations of Cooperation in Young Children', *Cognition* (108, 1, 222–231, 2008).

Rilling, J. K., D. A. Gutman, T. R. Zeh, G. Pagnoni, G. S. Berns and C. D. Kilts, 'A neural basis for social cooperation', *Neuron* (35, 395–405, 2002).

Rutherford, M. B., 'Children's autonomy and responsibility: An analysis of childrearing advice', *Qualitative Sociology* (32, 4, 337–353, 2009).

Thoits, P. and L. Hewitt, 'Volunteer work and well-being', *Journal of Health and Social Behavior* (42, 2, 115–131, 2001).

Warneken, F. and M. Tomasello, 'The roots of human altruism', *British Journal of Psychology* (100, 455–471, 2009).

Zukow-Goldring, P. G., 'Sibling caregiving', in M. H. Bornstein (ed.), *Handbook of parenting: Vol. 3. Status and social conditions of parenting* (177–208, Erlbaum, 1995).

THE MAGIC TOUCH

DeBenedet, A. T. and L. J. Cohen, *The Art of Roughhousing: Good Old-Fashioned Horseplay and Why Every Kid Needs It* (Quirk Books, 2010).

Dunbar, R. I. M., 'The social role of touch in humans and primates: Behavioural function and neurobiological mechanisms', *Neuroscience & Biobehavioral Reviews* (34, 260–268, 2010).

Gallace, A. and C. Spence, 'The science of interpersonal touch: An overview', *Neuroscience & Biobehavioral Reviews* (34, 246–259, 2010).

Harlow, H. F. and R. R. Zimmerman, 'Affectional responses in the infant monkey', *Science* (130, 421–432, 1959).

Hunziker, U. and R. Barr, 'Increased carrying reduces infant crying: A randomized controlled trial', *Pediatrics* (77, 5, 641–648, 1986).

Ishak, W. W., M. Kahloon and H. Fakhry, 'Oxytocin role in enhancing well-being: a literature review', *Journal of Affective Disorders* (130, 1, 1–9, 2011).

Jourard, S. M., 'An exploratory study of body accessibility', *British Journal of Social and Clinical Psychology* (5, 221–231, 1966).

Kemper, K. J. and E. A. Kelly, 'Treating children with therapeutic and healing touch', *Pediatric Annals* (33, 4, 248–252, 2004).

Nagasawa, M., S. Mitsui, S. En, N. Ohtani, M. Ohta, Y. Sakuma, T. Onaka, K. Mogi and T. Kikusui, 'Social evolution. Oxytocin-gaze positive loop and the coevolution of human-dog bonds', *Science* (348, 6232, 333–336, 2015).

So, P. S., Y. Jiang and Y. Qin, 'Touch therapies for pain relief in adults', *Cochrane Database of Systematic Reviews* (8, 4, CD006535, 2008).

Underdown, A., J. Barlow, V. Chung and S. Stewart-Brown, 'Massage intervention for promoting mental and physical health in infants aged under six months', *Cochrane Database of Systematic Reviews* (4, CD005038, 1996).

Uvnäs-Moberg, K., L. Handlin and M. Petersson, 'Self-soothing behaviors with particular reference to oxytocin release induced by non-noxious sensory stimulation', *Frontiers in Psychology* (5, 1529, 2015).

FINDING FLOW

Csikszentmihalyi, M., *Flow: The Psychology of Optimal Experience* (Harper and Row, 1990).

Csikszentmihalyi, M., 'Activity and happiness: Towards a science of occupation', *Journal of Occupational Science* (1, 1, 38–42, 1993).

Engeser, S. and F. Rheinberg, 'Flow, performance and moderators of challenge-skill balance', *Motivation and Emotion* (32, 3, 158–172, 2008).

Fullagar, C. J. and E. K. Kelloway, '"Flow" at work: an experience sampling approach', *Journal of Occupational and Organizational Psychology* (82, 595–615, 2009).

HAPPY CHOICES

Aknin, L. B., J. K. Hamlin and E. W. Dunn, 'Giving Leads to Happiness in Young Children', *PLoS One* (7(6): e39211. doi:10.1371/journal. pone.0039211, 2012)

Assor, A., H. Kaplan and G. Roth, 'Choice is good, but relevance is excellent: autonomy-enhancing and suppressing teacher behaviours predicting students' engagement in schoolwork', *British Journal of Educational Psychology* (72, 2, 261–278, 2002).

Deci, E. L., R. Koestner and R. M. Ryan, 'A meta-analytic review of experiments examining the effects of extrinsic rewards on intrinsic motivation', *Psychological Bulletin* (125, 6, 627–668, 1999).

Joussemet, M., R. Koestner, N. Lekes and N. Houlfort, 'Introducing uninteresting tasks to children: a comparison of the effects of rewards and autonomy support', *Journal of Personality* (72, 1, 139–166, 2004).

Miserandino, M., 'Children who do well in school: individual differences in perceived competence and autonomy in above-average children', *Journal of Educational Psychology* (88, 2, 203–214, 1996).

Schwartz, B., *The Paradox of Choice: Why More is Less* (Ecco, 2004).

Thaler, R. and C. Sunstein, *Nudge: Improving decisions about health, wealth, and happiness* (Yale University Press, 2008).

THE GREAT OUTDOORS

Barber, S. E., C. Jackson, S. Akhtar, D. D. Bingham, H. Ainsworth, C. Hewitt, G. Richardson, C. D. Summerbell, K. E. Pickett, H. J. Moore, A. C. Routen, C. L. O'Malley, S. Brierley and J. Wright, '"Pre-schoolers in the playground" an outdoor physical activity intervention for children aged 18 months to 4 years old: study protocol for a pilot cluster randomised controlled trial', *Trials* (9, 14, 326, 2013).

Berman, M. G., J. Jonides and S. Kaplan, 'The cognitive benefits of interacting with nature', *Psychological Science* (19, 12, 1207–1212, 2008).

Capaldi, C. A., R. L. Dopko and J. M. Zelenski, 'The relationship between nature connectedness and happiness: a meta-analysis', *Frontiers in Psychology* (5, 976, 2014).

Department of Health, Physical Activity, Health Improvement and Protection (2011). Start active, stay active: A report on physical activity from the four home countries' Chief Medical Officers. https://www.gov.uk/government/uploads/system/uploads/attachment_data/file/216370/dh_128210.pdf. Accessed 16 October 2015.

Groves, N. J., J. J. McGrath and T. H. Burne, 'Vitamin D as a neuro-steroid affecting the developing and adult brain', *Annual Review of Nutrition* (34, 117–141, 2014).

Herman, K. M., C. L. Craig, L. Gauvin and P. T. Katzmarzyk, 'Tracking of obesity and physical activity from childhood to adulthood: the physical activity longitudinal study', *International Journal of Pediatric Obesity* (4, 281–288, 2009).

Lee, K., K. Williams, L. Sargent, N. Williams and K. Johnson, '40-second green roof views sustain attention: The role of micro-breaks in attention restoration', *Journal of Environmental Psychology* (42, 182–189, 2015).

Louv, R., *Last Child in the Woods: Saving Our Children from Nature-Deficit Disorder* (Algonquin Books, 2005).

Lowry, C. A., J. H. Hollis, A. de Vries, B. Pan, L. R. Brunet, J. R. Hunt, J. F. Paton, E. van Kampen, D. M. Knight, A. K. Evans, G. A. Rook and S. L. Lightman, 'Identification of an immune-responsive mesolimbocortical serotonergic system: Potential role in regulation of emotional behavior', *Neuroscience* (146, 2, 756–772, 2007).

Raanaas, R., K. Evensen, D. Rich, G. Sjøstrøm and G. Patil, 'Benefits of indoor plants on attention capacity in an office setting', *Journal of Environmental Psychology* (31, 1, 99–105, 2011).

Shin, Y. H., H. J. Shin and Y. J. Lee, 'Vitamin D status and childhood health', *Korean Journal of Pediatrics* (56, 10, 417–423, 2013).

Thompson Coon, J., K. Boddy, K. Stein, R. Whear, J. Barton and M. H. Depledge, 'Does participating in physical activity in outdoor natural environments have a greater effect on physical and mental well-being than physical activity indoors? A systematic review', *Environmental Science and Technology* (45, 5, 1761–1772, 2011).

Tourula, M., A. Isola and J. Hassi, 'Children sleeping outdoors in winter: Parents' experiences of a culturally bound childcare practice', *International Journal of Circumpolar Health* (67, 2–3, 269–278, 2008).

Wells, N. M., 'At home with nature: Effects of "greenness" on children's cognitive functioning', *Environment and Behavior* (32, 6, 775–795, 2000).

Wells, N. M. and G. W. Evans, 'Nearby nature: A buffer of life stress among rural children', *Environment and Behavior* (35, 3, 311–330, 2003).

MINDFULNESS

Chiesa, A., R. Calati and A. Serretti, 'Does mindfulness training improve cognitive abilities? A systematic review of neuropsycho-logical findings', *Clinical Psychology Review* (31, 3, 449–464, 2011).

Flook, L., S. B. Goldberg, L. Pinger and R. J. Davidson, 'Promoting prosocial behavior and self-regulatory skills in preschool children through a mindfulness-based kindness curriculum', *Developmental Psychology* (51, 1, 44–51, 2015).

Keng, S. L., M. J. Smoski and C. J. Robins, 'Effects of mindfulness on psychological health: A review of empirical studies', *Clinical Psychology Review* (31, 6, 1041–1056, 2011).

Piet, J. and E. Hougaard, 'The effect of mindfulness-based cognitive therapy for prevention of relapse in recurrent major depressive disorder: A systematic review and meta-analysis', *Clinical Psychology Review* (31, 6, 1032–1040, 2011).

Tang, Y. Y., B. K. Hölzel and M. I. Posner, 'The neuroscience of mindfulness meditation', *Nature Reviews Neuroscience* (16, 4, 213–225, 2015).

Williams, M. and D. Penman, *Mindfulness: A Practical Guide to Finding Peace in a Frantic World* (Piatkus, 2011).

Zenner, C., S. Herrnleben-Kurz and H. Walach, 'Mindfulness-based interventions in schools – a systematic review and meta-analysis', *Frontiers in Psychology* (5, 603, 2014).

RECYCLING HAPPINESS

Angeles, L., 'Adaptation and anticipation effects to life events in the United Kingdom' (Scottish Institute for Research in Economics, 2010).

Lambert, N. M., A. M. Gwinn, R. F. Baumeister, A. Strachman, I. J. Washburn, S. L. Gable and F. D. Fincham, 'A boost of positive affect: The perks of sharing positive experiences', *Journal of Social and Personal Relationships* (30, 24–43, 2012).

La Rooy, D., M.-E. Pipe and J. E. Murray, 'Reminiscence and hyper-mnesia in children's eyewitness memory', *Journal of Experimental Child Psychology* (90, 235–254, 2005).

Nawijn, J., M. A. Marchand, R. Veenhoven and A. J. Vingerhoets, 'Vacationers happier, but most not happier after a holiday', *Applied Research in Quality of Life* (5, 35–47, 2010).

Wenner, J. A., M. M. Burch, J. S. Lynch and P. J. Bauer, 'Becoming a teller of tales: associations between children's fictional narratives and parent-child reminiscence narratives', *Journal of Experimental Child Psychology* (101, 1–19, 2008).

Index

365 Steps to Self-confidence

David Lawrence Preston

365 Steps to
Self-confidence
A complete programme for personal
transformation — in just a few minutes a day

David Lawrence Preston

Available to buy in ebook and paperback

Confidence is crucial to a happy and fulfilling life. And yet many of us lack confidence and self-belief. Each of the 52 sections contains information, insights and words of inspiration, plus seven exercises and practical hints or points to ponder. Fifteen minutes a day will give you tools and techniques which have worked for millions of people around the world. If you read the material carefully and apply what you learn, you really will notice big changes taking place within two or three months. A year from now you'll be amazed at how much more confident you've become.

Stress-Free Feeding: How to develop healthy eating habits in your child

Lucy Cooke and Laura Webber

Available to buy in ebook and paperback

A practical guide to feeding problems in children from 0 to 5, and how to solve them.

Using case studies and real-life examples, this book is full of sound expert advice on how best to feed your young children. It helps you understand the science, dispel the myths and see that other parents have similar concerns.

With hints and tips for each stage of feeding that will help develop healthy eating patterns for life, this book will put the pleasure back into family mealtimes.

Healthy Eating for Life

Robin Ellis

Available to buy in ebook and paperback

Easy-to-cook recipes for a healthier life

Eating healthily doesn't mean eating tastelessly - or having to follow a strict diet. Robin Ellis shows how, by simply choosing a Mediterranean approach to cooking, you can enjoy delicious food that is good for you.

Diagnosed with Type 2 diabetes, Robin was able to manage his condition for over six years without medication by following this eating style. Studies have also shown that a Mediterranean diet helps to maintain a healthy heart and to reduce the risk of dying from cancer.

- *Simple recipes that all the family can enjoy*
- *Make cooking an integral part of your life and take control of what you eat*
- *Feel long-term benefits, rejecting short-term diets*
- *Discover a balanced way of eating, avoiding extremes*